MW00891819

Copyright Info For How I Won The Battle:
Stories From Winning Women Anthology by
Visionary Dr. Freida Henderson

Created by Coach Tia Monique & Let It Out Academy©⊠
Linktr.ee/Coachtiamonique

ABOUT THE VISIONARY

Depression. Domestic abuse. Divorce. These are but a few of the adversities that Dr. Freida Henderson has boldly broken down. Fueled by a strong sense of faith and courage, this brave woman of God shows us the power that just one individual can make in the lives of many.

Dr. Freida Henderson is the Senior Pastor and Founder of Greater Word of Truth in Raleigh, North Carolina. As an apostolic visionary, this woman of God has also birthed Women of Destiny Fellowship, Faith Assembly Christian Academy, Faith Assembly Christian Child Development Center, and New Beginnings School of Etiquette and Excellence. Through these ministries, God has allowed her to impact her community and surrounding areas.

Dr. Freida Henderson is a woman after God's own heart that has been in ministry for over twenty-three years. Her ministry training includes youth and choir director in Upper Heyford, England, as well as Armor bearer, youth minister, and usher. God uses her in the anointing of the worshiping arts, training in the areas of dance, mime, and the penning of inspirational books and writings.

She operates under the covering of Bethel Family Worship Center headquartered in Durham, North Carolina, where the presiding Bishop George G. Bloomer serves as the Senior Pastor.

Dr. Freida Henderson has an anointing to lead those held captive by the enemy out of the clutches by implementing practical teaching and wisdom life lessons. She has a heart for those that are broken and hurting, sharing them God's message of love and hope. She is known as a prolific preacher and teacher.

Operating in the Five Fold Ministry, God is using her to carry out her designated assignment "building people." Dr. Freida Henderson has extended her ministry with her unit Freida's Victorious Achievers. Her main goal is to empower others to achieve financial stability through entrepreneurship. Moreover, she is a successful entrepreneur having owned and operated Memories by Freida, a Bible bookstore, author of Incredible Confessions of a Winner, The Winning Approach, and Speak To My Heart!

Dr. Freida has released four Spoken Word Gospel Music CD's, "So You Would Know…", this unique record complete with full musical composition has gained the attention of consumers and radio announcers throughout NC in its first few months of release. Her other spoken word cd's include, Take My Word Healing Scripture, Take My Word Faith Scripture CD and Incredible Confessions of a Winner: Dynamic Winning Confessions! Her inspiration to record a spoken word project resulted in a nomination of "Female Vocalist of the Year, and was recognized at TCP Magazines 9th Anniversary "You Don't Know My Story" 2013's Overcoming Women!

Dr. Frieda has launched her You Tube channel "Women Ready 2 Win." This station was not just for women, but men as well. In October of 2013, she had "60 Seconds with Apostle", where she gave weekly messages of encouragement and guidance to listeners on the Steve Harvey radio station, 96.9 BZJ before it was removed from the area.

She is a highly sought-after motivational speaker, life coach, and multi-business owner. Dr. Freida was selected to speak on the Leadership Experience Tour, led by Shawn Fair, on the #1 speaking platform in the US. She's also been recognized by FOX, NBC, ABC, and other media outlets.

As a successful entrepreneur, she provides her clients with a framework and safe environment to build confidence, conquer fears, and manifest their dreams. She has also founded Freida's Victorious Achievers, an initiative to empower others to achieve financial stability through entrepreneurship.
She is a licensed Esthetician.

While enduring situations that appeared most challenging to the ordinary, Dr. Freida has proven to defy the odds of not allowing challenges to overtake her. She has risen to live beyond what life has served her. She applies the fertilizer from her past traumas to flourish the lives of others. As life engages trials and tribulations, Dr. Freida inspires others to adopt her winning approach to life.

Dr. Henderson has dedicated her life to winning souls and saving lives for Jesus Christ. She is the spiritual mother to hundreds of sons and daughters. Apostle Freida Henderson is also the biological mother of three beautiful children Anthony, Jelisa, and Charles and the proud grandmother of five beautiful granddaughters Sumaya, Kameron, Dakota, and Kalli, Kasside and her grandson Zaire.

Connect with Dr. Freida at https://thewinningapproach.com.

ACKNOWLEDGEMENTS

I am beyond grateful for the love, support and encouragement from my three wonderful children Anthony Jelisa and Charles. They have always been my biggest cheerleaders, always pushing me to pursue my dreams and overcome any obstacles in my way. Their unwavering belief in me has been a constant source of motivation and inspiration reminding me why I do what I do. It is with immense pride and joy that I acknowledge them in my new book. Thank you all for being the Wind Beneath My Wings.

Coach Tia Monique, thank you, thank you, thank you! Your support, encouragement and push have been instrumental in helping me become the Entrepreneur I am today. Not only have you poured into me, you've also pulled out of me gifts that I never knew existed. You have helped me to realize my full potential and have inspired me to do great things in my own life. I am grateful to our Heavenly Father for placing you in my life to help me on my journey. Your prayers have also been a source of comfort and strength for me. Coach Tia, you are truly anointed for what you do and I cannot express my gratitude enough.

Greater Word of Truth, your support and love has been a constant source of strength for me. I cannot thank you enough for always being there to encourage and uplift me. Your support has enabled me to achieve great things and accomplish what I once thought was impossible. I am honored to be your Apostle and to have such an incredible congregation. You all are truly a blessing from God and I am forever grateful to have such a supportive church family.

It brings me so much joy to express my gratitude to the amazing women who entrusted me with their stories in my first anthology. Your bravery and willingness to step out on faith and share your experiences of overcoming adversities, disappointments and abuse is truly inspiring.

As your Winning Coach, I feel Blessed to have played a part in your journey towards becoming authors and successful business women. For those of you who are first time authors, congratulations on this incredible accomplishment. Your lives are forever changed by this milestone, and I have no doubt that your stories will touch the lives of others and bring healing deliverance and freedom. You are all true Overcomers and I am honored to have worked with you.

Dr. Freida Henderson

TABLE OF CONTENTS

CHAPTER 1

Behind The Looking Glass
By
Danielle Adams

I'm sure some things that happened in my childhood are relatable and some things aren't. When I started writing my chapter, I initially started at the point I am currently in my life. Then I realized, even for me, to understand who I am now, you must know what I experienced in my past. So, I had to go back to the beginning. Imagine being a child at the age of 8, the oldest, and charged with being responsible for making sure your soon to be 4-year-old sister was taken care of and didn't get into any trouble. If anything happens to her while you're around, you're going to be in trouble. That's what was told to me numerous times.

My mom and dad played softball for a local league and were often away playing ball and/or partying on the weekends, so we were often left with a babysitter on the weekends my grandma couldn't keep us. The older lady that kept us was a family friend who lived in an older house. In her home, it was her, her granddaughter, and her grown son.
At that time the granddaughter was around 13 or 14 years of age. When we were there, the babysitter used to make us stay outside all day, as was the norm back then.

From morning to night, we were outside.
At night we would come in, eat dinner and bathe and then go straight to bed. In the house, there were two bedrooms. One upstairs, where the son slept, and one downstairs, where the babysitter, the granddaughter, and my sister and I slept. In that bedroom, there were two beds, a twin and a double. The babysitter slept in the twin, and we slept in the double.
Imagine waking up in the middle of the night, at the age of 8, to another female with their face between your legs and their mouth and tongue on your private parts. My mama told me that if I let anybody touch, she was going to beat me until I had no skin left. Remember that part, cause it's important.

When the granddaughter realized I was waking up, she hurried up and put her hands over my mouth and told me if I made any noise her grandmother was going to wake up and beat me. I didn't want to get in trouble. Back then, my mama used to tell us that if we got in trouble at the babysitter's, the babysitter had permission to whoop us, and we would get another whooping when we got home.

So, I just laid there. And this continued for several weeks. It got to the point where I would beg my parents to let us stay at home. That I would protect and watch over my sister. But they wouldn't let us stay at home. So yeah, I would just deal with whatever.
Then came tournament weekend. My parents were leaving on that Thursday morning and weren't coming back until Sunday. This was the time that I felt that all hell broke loose for me.

We were dropped off at the babysitter's that Thursday morning. And any other time the granddaughter was cordial, nice really and fun to be around. She was popular with the neighborhood kids. Especially the boys. How ironic, huh!?! This day, I remember her being so mean to me and my sister. Calling us names and she even hit me one time during a game we were playing, because I missed a jump. She was angry all day. I still remember that day like yesterday, even at the age of 46. Everything else about that day was the same routine. When the sun went down, we came in and ate dinner and bathed and went to bed.

As time went on, I was just lying there waiting for something to happen, but it never did, so eventually I fell asleep. Then, I was jolted out of my sleep by her telling me to put my mouth on her like she had been doing me!! Say what!?! I told her no, I don't want to. She then said to me, oh, so you have been enjoying me doing you all this time, but you don't want to do me. In my mind, I was like I haven't been enjoying anything, but I didn't want to get in trouble.

I never verbally responded to her, but she could see the look on my face. So, then she said, well, if you don't do it, I'll get your sister to. Remember my little sister was 4 years old and my mama said I would be in trouble if anything happened to her. To me it felt like a lot of pressure on my hands. Either way I was in trouble, but I knew that my mama would kill me if something happened to my sister.

At this point there was nothing for me to do, but to do it. So, this was the first time I let my mind go blank. I didn't think about what I was doing, I just did it. Out of mind, out of body experience. All I knew was that I had to protect my sister at any cost. And I now realize that the cost I paid was a part of my mental stability. If I had said something, I just felt like the babysitter wouldn't believe my word against her granddaughter.

This went on for about a year, until my parents decided we could stay home by ourselves. Life was a little easier. For a few years anyway. My parents stopped playing ball, but now they were gambling. On Fridays they were the house that hosted and on Saturdays and Sundays someone else hosted at their place. The weekends were my most peaceful times.

Why? Because my parents made us stay in our rooms, unless we had to use the bathroom or come out to get some of that good ol' fried chicken, that my daddy would cook while they hosted all these men and women, mostly men.

These people would be at the house all night long and then leave in the morning to go on to the next place. When my parents left on Saturdays it would be such a relief that I didn't even care that we had to clean up the mess that was left behind. I just wanted the peace of mind of being left alone.

By this time, I was 10 about to be 11. My body had started maturing in some areas, and I guess as much as I was told to stay in my bedroom, during those quick visits to the kitchen and bathroom, I started to catch the eyes of some of the men that would come to the house.

I remember one Saturday after everyone had left the house, the doorbell rang. My sister was in her room, and I was in the kitchen cleaning up. I peeped around the corner to look in the driveway to see if the car was familiar and if I could tell who it was at the door. Because you already know, I wasn't supposed to be opening the door period point blank anyway.

But I looked and recognized the car as somebody that would come to the house every Friday to play cards and that he was also a friend. So, I opened the door thinking that maybe he had forgotten something and had come back to get it. Yeah, that was not the case.

There this man was standing at the door with money in his hand. He started by saying how pretty I was and that I had a cute little body. He then said, I'll pay you $25 a week if you just let me kiss your private area. Of course, he didn't describe it in that manner, but you get the point. I just shut the door in his face. I was super scared. The storm door always kept us separated.

When I shut the door, he started yelling. Talking about you better not say anything or you're going to be in trouble. Now remember I said earlier that my mama said that she would beat me until the skin came off if I let someone touch any of my private areas, and I believed her.

And here I was again, in a situation, where that very thing was in question. He even said, if you don't tell, I'll give you the $25 the next time you see me. I just better not say anything. Well, he didn't have to worry about me saying anything, cause once again it would have been my fault for opening the door. Never mind the fact that a grown man that they welcomed into their house had the audacity to make an offer to someone he knew to be a minor.

He did give me the $25 the next time he saw me. However, the request did not stop. Every week he would find some way to proposition me. Every time I would say no, and he continued to give me the money anyway to keep me from telling.

Now, after a few times, I tried to bring it up to my mama, in a roundabout way, but I would never just come right out and tell her or my daddy for that matter. I was too scared. So, I kept collecting the money. Then one day, he doubled the money and offered me $50 to let him do the same thing that he had originally asked for.

By this point, I can't even lie. I had thought about giving in, but something kept pulling me back. And I'm so thankful I didn't, because he died years later from AIDS. Even though it was years after the incidents, no one could really say how long he had the disease. Even when we don't think about God watching over and protecting us, He is. He's always on watch and providing His hedge of protection.

I'm going to stop that story right there. I could continue for days, and one day I may tell the whole story from beginning to end. But I wanted to share that part of my life, because as hard and as evil as I thought that was then, I realize that the way that the world is today, that living a young and carefree life is harder, and to some unimaginable. Behind the smiles of our young people, we don't see the hurt or the pain, even the fear that they have just trying to survive throughout the course of the day.

We are so quick to say that times have changed, and yes, they have. But the one thing that should always stay the same, regardless of how things are, is communication. Not having the open pathway to communicate, effectively and without fear, your thoughts and emotions can cause more damage than being able to express yourself freely. Even as adults, we still find this simple act difficult at times, so imagine the mind and the rationale of a child who fears their parents.

Our offspring deserve so much more than the world is giving them. Yes, times were different when I was growing up and some subjects were taboo. But now, there should be no excuse and no reason that our young people should have to feel like they cant come to us and tell us their deepest thoughts, feelings and emotions. In some areas, the world has made it acceptable for our youth to think that they have no one to talk to.

That it's acceptable to keep the things that hurt and bother them up on the inside. Because showing any type of emotions, that represent the hurt or the sadness in their life, may represent or portray them as being weak; when showing those emotions and releasing the things that are bothering them speaks of strength.

While I may be focusing on our youth and young adults, we must also remember that there are more seasoned adults that are still dealing with and suffering from things that happened in their childhood. I know for me, for years, I didn't know if I really liked men or if I liked females. I struggled with thinking I liked females, but I know that according to the Bible that that wasn't right. I even engaged in a 3-year relationship with a female.

And while I enjoyed that relationship, I felt like there was a piece of me that didn't quite fall into place and I knew then that being with females was not a part of my makeup, but it took years for me to realize this. Even being a young married woman with a child.

I shared all of that because, we as humans, and supposedly mature adults, are so quick to judge others about their lifestyles. I'm guilty of this too, without knowing how and why people act the way that they do. How someone may react with fright at a simple touch. How someone's energy turns to nervousness when someone places a hand on their shoulder. How a person looks like they are almost in tears because someone has innocently leaned over to whisper something in their ear. How a person who sleeps in the bed alone, only sleeps on the very edge, so that they don't feel like they could be trapped while they are sleeping.

How a person that presents to the public a strong and sometimes unbending personality, but on the inside it's because they are struggling to hold on to some of the power, just a little of the power that they have worked so hard to regain, that they feel can be taken from them at the drop of a hat. WE just never know what has transpired in a person's life to make them act and react the way they do.

Now while I am comfortable enough now to tell a part of this story, I still struggle on a daily basis. I question myself about who I am as a person, what are my true desires and wants? What are the things I really need to live and succeed in life? These are questions that consistently swirl through my head. The shining light through all of this is that even on my loneliest, lowest and most confused days, GOD stayed with me through it all and he never gave up on me.

I want the readers to understand that there is more behind the looking glass than they will ever see in others' lives. A little kindness and understanding goes a long way. And even if you don't fully understand the situation, sometimes the thing that is really needed is a listening ear, compassion and an open heart.

BIO

I am a mother of one adult son, Nelson Hill, who I love more then he will ever know. Divorced for a year after being married for 26 years. So, I've had to learn how to start over on my own. While I will admit that this journey has not been easy, it's been worth it for my peace of mind and sanity. I currently work for a major insurance company and am the owner of 4 successful businesses; Savoree Creations, Couponing and Coffee, Tiffany Travels, and Negi Holdings.

I thank God for them because they allow me to express my talents in several different areas and gave me something to focus on after my divorce. I currently reside in Raleigh, where I've lived for 16 years. I grew up in a time where secrets were kept and taken to the grave.

Those secrets that went to the grave still had the power to effect how family members interacted with others and how people continued to act. Being able to be a part of this assembly of work, has indeed been a great honor for me and I count it an accomplishment to be able to share a part of my story in the hopes that whoever reads this collection of awesome and phenomenal stories, by these ladies that shared a piece of their heart, will be able to continue to break the cycle of holding on to secrets that continues to damage families.

MUCH LOVE

Danielle Adams

SPONSORED BREAK

S.A.C APPAREL & EMBROIDERY

One can find a variety of uniform wholesale
selection & customizations.

Categories to include:
Medical, Cosmetology, Culinary Arts and more.

At S&E we like to go the extra mile to
achieve your business goals and
provide a conducive service that will
set them up for Success!

CHAPTER 2

God's Plans Will Always Override Life's Circumstances

By

Dr. Cynthia Whaley

The pandemic of 2020 taught me to be more grateful for everyday simple things and encounters. Living life is beautiful and should be embraced with maximum zeal. This has been my perception since my youth. Although I grew up in poverty, I still enjoyed matching unusual patterns and colors together, producing a bold fashion statement. Fashion has a special place in the fiber of my being. For me, styling is therapeutic and artistically creative. After high school, I entered college and worked as a babysitter for my departmental dean. I also worked as a clerk at a local grocery store chain in order to earn extra cash.

I was a typical college student and enjoyed going to the mall. Still today, mall shopping is a special activity and much enjoyed.

One summer afternoon in 1994, I was on one of my shopping trips at a local mall when I met a young, hazel-eyed United States marine. His physique was that of a masterpiece and his voice was distinct and fulfilling. I literally thought Heaven had been transported to the local mall. A conversation was ignited and soon phone numbers were exchanged in the initial meeting. After numerous phone calls over the course of a week, we went out on our first date to dinner and movies. Soon after, emotions burst and took over, which led to a breathtaking, loving courtship. I literally put everything that I had learned about Jesus up on a shelf.

By this time, I had received my Associate of Arts degree and was pursuing my Bachelor of Arts degree. The courtship became more intense and progressed rapidly. Against God's will, my parents' will and my beliefs, I moved in with this man that had me mesmerized.

Yes, I shacked up and enjoyed every minute of myself indulging in sin. Even in my backsliding, God still had a plan for my life that would eventually be fulfilled. In January of 1995, my boyfriend and I were united in holy matrimony.

In the spring of the following year, we purchased our first home in a very desirable neighborhood. My husband continued to serve his country while I earned my Bachelor of Arts degree with honors. Within a matter of months, I entered the workforce and began to excel in my criminal justice career. Life was amazing, so I thought. I was living life on my own terms. We were looked at as a couple who had it all! To me we had it all, except for a child. We had tried for many years to no avail. It was during this time that I rededicated my life back to Christ in May of 1995.

To date, this was the best decision I ever made. I have been running for Jesus ever since. I was married and Holy Ghost filled. Yet, I still had goals and I pursued my graduate degree and earned it in May 2001. Fast forward, life continues to get better for us, but still no child. Remember, like I said in the beginning, God had a plan. As His children, we must know there is no expiration date on the promise. Waiting in faith is a part of the process. Faith involves belief in the process without the evidence in the natural.

I continued believing against all odds for a child. The Bible lets us know that faith is the substance of things hoped for, the evidence of things not seen. I would have visions of me holding a baby girl. God just gave me a glimpse of my promise. Each month I hoped I would receive the good news that I was pregnant. I could see a baby with my spiritual eyes, but nothing was produced in the natural. Still, I had a vision that just would not die. In the process of waiting on the promise, you must believe 100% that God is going to do it.

Negative self-doubt can abort your seed and promise. Your faith is supercharged with belief. Perhaps some things in your life have not manifested yet, simply due to negative beliefs. There's manifestation power in your belief in God. Use it in every area, and every trail of your life. You, too, will see how success increases in your life. Learn how to succeed off your faith in God.

My faith was stronger than my understanding. When you believe this way, you will supersede all earthly logic. Up to this point all my older sisters had sons, but I knew I would eventually have a daughter. In the fall of 2003, I abruptly became sick with a terrible cold. I couldn't eat, was lightheaded. and stayed out of work for three days. While at home, I rested in bed and my husband said to me, "if you are sick tomorrow, I'm taking you to the emergency room", and he did just that. Remember, my belief in having a daughter was still in play.

Originally, I thought my bad cold had progressed to the flu. After labs were drawn, it was concluded I was pregnant. Look at God! From diagnosis of a cold to shifting to the promise: final diagnosis of a baby! That's exactly how God shifts when we believe Him.

We should believe God over systems, luck, numbers, and Science. Belief against all hope is what it takes to see the promise. Believe the words of the Lord, and the promises spoken over your life and situation. With Jesus having all power in His hands, you cannot help but win! That's right, with Jesus you have a winning hand!

My pregnancy was difficult. When you are carrying the promise, when you are carrying the gift, when you are carrying the anointing, don't think it's going to be easy. It's not a walk in the park or the breezeway. The greatest is always covered in pain and suffering! God gives his greatest soldiers the difficult assignments to carry and deliver. I went on bed rest in the third month. By the fourth month, my unborn daughter was diagnosed with spina bifida. During the fifth month I went into premature labor. Fortunately, it was controlled. Throughout my pregnancy, I had severe nausea and chronic vomiting until I delivered my daughter. By the eighth month, her organs were underweight.

During my entire pregnancy I only gained five pounds. Through it all I stayed focused on not only carrying but delivering the promise. If you are going through a difficult moment, see yourself on the other side. Know that God cares about you and everything that involves you. Everyday, affirm and say to yourself: "I am a deliverer." Remember faith is not a feeling, but a belief; knowing that Jesus is going to see you through into a better place called victory. In April 2004, after 36 hours of labor, I delivered a 5 pounds 4 ounces baby girl. Your faith executes your wishes, when you don't quit amidst your pain!

My life was complete, and I had a deeper love for God. As years passed, my marriage weakened and eventually demised and ended in divorce after 13 years. I am so thankful for my promise—my daughter gives me love which strengthens me daily. She was almost two when my divorce was final. When you start a new relationship—start it right: the beginning affects the foundational stability. Shacking is never the right answer and God frowns upon sin. Furthermore, sin separates us from God. Let us keep the faith and know that God has crafted a mate just for you. There is a spiritual equation called reaping and sowing. Plant good godly seeds in your relationship so it can grow to maturity.

Keep living and breathing faith, while voiding out negativity, doubt and naysayers' comments. Life moves on and I am embracing my singleness. When my daughter was three, she began to get sick often. I made sure she had the best medical care, topped with lots of love and spoiling moments.

Although her parents divorced, we had one thing in common:
we both loved our daughter, and we were there for her.

To this day my daughter is 18 and she still has both of her parents' love and support.
My ex-husband gave me a gift I could never give to myself alone: my daughter.
When your faith is in an overriding mode you can look at every situation and see the good!
One morning I woke up and saw my daughter was paralyzed in her face.

I immediately called her pediatrician, and an afternoon appointment was set. We arrived at the doctor's office, checked in and waited for the doctor. The doorknob turned, the doctor sat on the stool, looked at my daughter, listened to her vitals, stepped outside the room and then re-entered the room to tell me to immediately take my daughter to the emergency room. I knew something was wrong because of the look on the doctor's face. I was told my daughter needed further testing. When I arrived at Le Bonheur Children's Hospital, Memphis, Tennessee, I checked my daughter in and within one minute they were examining my daughter.

Next a team of white coat doctors began asking me questions and they immediately took my daughter to the trauma unit. Wait, I was confused. What's going on? I was all alone; there was a gunshot patient in trauma whose brain had swelling, so I knew my daughter's situation was critical. No God, not my only child! Then the doctors delivered the news. My daughter's kidney was damaged and failing her. The doctors explained that they don't want it to progress to stage four, which was complete kidney failure.

This was unbelievable, and after we arrived at the hospital her body began to shut down. God, God where are you? I lost my husband due to divorce and now my daughter is gravely ill. Oh Lord, help me! I paused and thought I was having a bad dream. I told the doctors to call me and provide updates. I went home and got in my bed. It really seemed like a bad dream. I woke up the following morning to the doctors calling me. I was provided an update about her night.

She was in the Intensive Care Unit, and it was so hard for me to ring the bell and walk through the double doors and see my sweet little four-year-old daughter fighting for her life. But when I went home the previous night, I cried out to the Lord, and He endowed me with all I needed to care for my daughter. Due to her kidney failing, she was swollen beyond recognition. I can remember looking at the patient's name on the end of her bed because she did not look like my daughter. Yes, I paused; but I did not quit!

Pausing means I am not putting forth any of my efforts: God I surrender all to you! This situation that I was facing was too big for me to handle in my human element. When I couldn't, God did the impossible! Jehovah Rapha was dispatched and within nine days, my daughter went into a regular room! When something is paused it eventually resumes. It's okay to pause and get heavenly strategies and then resume accordingly.

I slept night after night in a chair at my daughter's bedside with the belief that God was going to heal her in his own way and God did just that! Let your belief be so strong that you say: "not my will but your will be done, Heavenly Father." Believe in God's will and God's provision for your life. Let go and let God navigate you to victory. Trust Him with your whole heart and you will see life brought back to dead situations.

Now my daughter was in a regular room and her body was strong enough to get dialysis. Keep lodged in your memory that we are talking about a four-year-old. She was well-mannered and the toughest kid that I knew. Dialysis worked well on her body in the hospital. Next, I planned for continuous home dialysis. I went through intense training so I could administer peritoneal dialysis. I also learned how to give Epogen shots. Epogen is a blood thinner given to renal patients. I was so happy, I did it and one month later my daughter went from the grave to our house!

She could not check out on life because God had a greater plan for her life. Your life is in the palm of God's hand, and you are set up for the greatest win of your life. It's not the giant but it's the giant slayer inside of you! In August of 2008, I enrolled her into kindergarten, and she started school on time! Remember, your life forges ahead after a pause, with God leading you every step of the way. Now I have the grace to understand my daughter's sickness and we are living life on our terms. She went to school every day, played and did her homework.

The highlight of her day was when I would fix her hair. She loved satin ribbons and bows. I would connect her up to the machine nightly. She would cry every night because the pull would hurt her muscles. When she was connected to the machine, I would put her on my lap and gently shake her to lessen the pain. After the first cycle, my father would call her and encourage her. His voice was calming and brought my daughter peace. We must learn how to celebrate each of our wins because Satan comes to kill, steal, and destroy.

March of my daughter's kindergarten year emerged. She began to get sick, and her dialysis was not working well. She was hospitalized for almost two months and during this time she was put on the kidney transplant list. She was released from the hospital. Five days later I received the phone call that informed us that a match had been found for my daughter and we must get to the hospital immediately. This was Monday and by night around 6:48pm they rolled my daughter in the operating room for a kidney transplant; another life-saving surgery. I paused again. I cried, I literally couldn't walk to the surgery room—it was unexplainable! I watched as they pushed her down the hallway slowly; not knowing the outcome.

Lord knows I paused; it felt like my life was leaving me. I just couldn't walk. I returned to her regular room and at 1:07am the surgeon came and told me that the surgery went well, and I could see my daughter! She was in the Intensive Critical Care Unit, and I walked down with the surgeon and my heart rejoiced! No, she didn't know it was me; but she was alive. I paused but God didn't. I paused but God worked overtime!

On May 27, 2022, my daughter had her second kidney transplant. She graduated from high school on June 4th. School administrators gave her high school diploma while she was on her hospital bed. My daughter did the convocation at her high school graduation through her cellphone while lying on her hospital bed. She graduated with honors, was the top female senior of the year, captain of the quiz bowl and robotic club, and she earned a full-ride academic scholarship. There are too many accolades, achievements to name.

Just know God's plan is greater than any suffering you'll ever deal with in life. Today, she is a freshman at Winston State University. She has plans on becoming a lawyer. Surely there is a mighty call upon her life. Complicated births always produce the never seen before anointing. Remember our Lord and Savior Jesus the Christ's birth. Look at what He Did! Pausing is part of the process. Just don't forget to press the resume button. God is turning your calamity into a victory. What makes a sweet victory is an almost defeat. My faith kept me strong; my belief allowed me to see results. I paused and Jesus prepared the way.

My daughter, Mallory, is alive and well today! She survived Covid-19, cancer and two transplants. Why? Because her call is greater than her sickness. God's plans will always override life's circumstances.

BIO

Dr Cynthia Whaley has an intense passion for God. She has heard a clarion call upon her life. Her assignment is to build up the downtrodden with the Word of the Lord through the process of exhortation.She is the third daughter of William and Elder Linda Washington.
She was born and raised in Lenoir County and has been preaching the gospel of Jesus Christ for over 20 years.

In 2018, she birthed Destiny Walker Mentoring Ministry, which empowers others to walk boldly into their destiny. The prophetic in her instructs many business owners.She is affectionately known among them as "the birthing mother." She is the chief executive officer of Kingdom Flow Marketing Firm, which provides strategic marketing too small to medium-size ministries.

Currently, she is enrolled at Liberty University, finishing her doctoral studies in Psychology. It is her desire to impact not only Christendom but; the world with the transformation of God's love and power. She has been employed with North Carolina State government over two decades and currently is a full-time faculty member at the community college level. From an academia perspective, she enjoys studying and conducting mixed research methodology with a concentration in empirical analysis of psychological empowerment.

God has blessed the fruit of her labor, and this is her third anthology/co-author project. She believes writing has a way of releasing on paper what God is sharing in the Spirit realm. Simply put, the inspiration of God's words releases strength when we read.
From an author perspective, she is transparent and knows the words written offer solutions and healing mechanisms.

In 2022, she graduated from Kingdom Perspective Institute as a certified life coach. Additionally, she is known as the "empowerment-pusher" and provides life-changing strategies and solutions infused with biblical principles during her coaching session. She is a spiritual daughter of Global Ministry Center International and received an Honorary Doctor of Divinity from Great Commission Bible College.

In her leisure time, she enjoys traveling, fashion, business seminars, and fine dining. She is married to Reverend Vincent Whaley, who has stood by her side since the inception of their courtship.Together they are raising their youngest daughter, Mallory, a college junior majoring in Political Science. Academics is at the forefront of Mallory's agenda; God blessed her with a full-ride academic scholarship. Above all, Dr. Whaley wants you to know that putting God first will transform your life, into an abundance of victories.

SPONSORED BREAK

CHAPTER 3

How To Overcome Abuse & Pain

By
Rosetta Campbell

Wow. Who would have thought that I would have ended up in a situation like this? My whole life was turned upside down. Mesmerized by those brown eyes and that sexy charm. Thinking that I had a good thing going, when I fell in love with someone that I thought was going to be my king. It was all a wakeup call.

For the first few months that we dated, everything was good, at least until we started having kids together. I had my second child from him in the summer of '93 (his first, my second). About a month after my daughter was born, I had to go downtown to get her social security card, so that I could have it for important paperwork. My kids and I caught the bus downtown. We spent almost an hour waiting for someone to call my name to fill out the paperwork and to get the ball rolling.

After I got everything done, I called my oldest daughters' father to see if he was home so that he could see her. My second daughters' father was not too fond of him, so I had to sneak over to his house just so he could see his daughter. We got to her dad's house at about 3:30 that afternoon and we left there at about 5:30 that evening. As we were getting closer to home, I was trying to think of some real good lie to tell, because I knew he would be a little upset.

When I got into the house, he was there sitting on the couch and he started asking me where I had been all day. I told him that I was downtown handling business for our daughter. He was like no you weren't, because the place closes at 5:00, so he kept questioning me and I was getting tired of it. I told him that I took my child to see her father and then he started putting his finger against my head and I kept moving it.

Then, he pushed me up against the front door and said, "You had my daughter in that darn heat all day long at some other man's house?" I responded, 'no, we were not in the heat, we were in the house'. Lord, why did I say that? The next thing I know his fist connected to my eye. I dropped to my knees. I was in shock. I couldn't believe that he had done that to me, with my daughter standing right there. When I got up off the floor, I took my children upstairs to get them ready for dinner and then a bath.

As I was in the bathroom, I looked in the mirror and my jaw was so swollen it looked like I had a tooth pulled or something and my eye was blood shot red. I was so hurt. After a few hours passed he tried to apologize to me and said that he didn't mean to do it and that it will never happen again. I believed the lie and forgave him.

The next day I got up and went to check on the kids. They were still asleep, so I went downstairs to get breakfast started. As I was walking into the kitchen, I heard a knock on the door. I was like who in the world could that be? I went to the door to look out of the peep hole to see who it was. It was my best friend who lived right around the corner from us. I was like oh my God why is she here on this day and why not a few days from now? I didn't want to open the door because I was so ashamed and embarrassed, but she kept knocking and eventually I opened the door.

When I opened the door and she saw my face she was like, what happened to your face? I was like, I hit myself in the face with the door. She was like no you didn't, don't lie to me, tell me the truth. I was like, for real I did. Then she said girl stop lying, he hit you didn't he? And I said yes in a low voice because I didn't want him to hear me telling her. She told me to go take out charges against him, but I said no and that it would never happen again.

That next year I had another child, a little boy. Things had gotten a lot worse. I was not able to communicate with my family. I really didn't have any friends. With the ones I had, we would gossip about each other and our relationships. About six months after having my son, I found out that he was cheating with someone in the neighborhood. I was very angry about that. He would stay out all night and when he would come in and I would ask him where he was, he would say with the boys. I knew he was lying.

So, I asked him about the lady he was cheating on me with and that started an argument and a fight. This time I was fighting back, at least I tried until he grabbed me and started choking me to the point that I was gasping for air. Every time we would argue he would say things like 'nobody wants you' or 'if you want to leave, go ahead and leave but the kids are staying here'. He would cuss me out and get all up in my face. I was so scared, but I didn't want him to have my children, so I stayed. When he would calm down, he would still apologize and lie and I kept believing them every time. We would be intimate, and I would get pregnant every time.

This time, during this pregnancy, I was having some complications. I was having labor pains at 6mos of pregnancy. The doctors stopped my labor and kept me in the hospital for about a day. They told me that they wanted me to carry the baby to at least 7 and a half months, at least that would give him a fighting chance. I was so stressed out and worried about my baby and my other kids.

When I got out of the hospital, I had to be on bed rest for a little while, but that didn't last long at all. Still found myself doing everything around the house while he was out cheating again. This time with a young lady in high school that was about to graduate. His sister introduced them. And being that she didn't have a date for the prom, that's what he told me. Me being naïve I was like 'ok' thinking that it was just for a prom. He said that he only did it for his sister. So, he ended up meeting her parents and taking her to the prom. Little did I know it was going to be more than just a date to the prom.

That morning when he came home, I was up with the kids. I asked him where he had been, and he said that he went to his friend's house after dropping her off at home and that they started talking and drinking, so he stayed the night at his house. For some reason I felt deep down that it was a lie, so I continued to press the issue and ask him was he with her? He kept saying no. I told him that he was lying and that he needed to leave.

I started packing his stuff as I was packing his stuff, he grabbed me, pushed me on the bed and pinned me down and yelled in my face that he is not going anywhere. If anybody was going to be leaving, it would be me. I told him no he had to go because I was tired of his lies and cheating and abuse. He told me again that he wasn't going anywhere and for me to stop telling him to get out. After he let me go, he got in the bed to go to sleep, while I was left standing there crying, hurt and angry, because I just wanted him to go.

As the months went by, he somehow continued to see this young lady long after the prom. Around September there was a commercial on tv about the state fair. I wanted to take the kids when it came in October. When he came home that day, I asked him if we could all go to the fair and he said yes. The only thing was that I couldn't ride on anything because I was pregnant. I just wanted to go eat and let the kids enjoy themselves. So, when October came and it was the day of the fair, we were ready to go. I kept calling him and calling him to see if he was on his way to pick us up.

He never answered until it was already dark and cool outside. By that time, I had put the kids to bed. I was so hurt because I wanted the kids to go have a good time. After I got the kids settled, I started to feel contractions, they were light to moderate ones, but I knew they were there. It was too early for me to go into labor. So, I laid down on my bed just so that they could ease off, but they didn't. I called his sister to see if she could get up with him because I couldn't after I had just spoken to him a few hours ago. She knew where he was and who he was with.

When he got to the house, I was already in full labor and ready to go to the hospital. My neighbor came over to watch the kids for us so that we could leave. That night I gave birth to a beautiful baby boy. He was 4 lbs and strong. He stayed in the hospital until he gained some weight and was able to be off the oxygen. After about a month in the hospital, he was able to come home. I was so happy about that.

In December of that same year, tragedy happened. I put my kids to bed at about 9pm. I remember getting up to feed my son and then putting him back to bed after feeding and changing him. When I woke up the next morning to check on the kids, I noticed that he was still sleeping. At least that's what I thought until I went over to pick him up and his lips were purple and he was not breathing. I ran out of the room with him in my arms and into my bedroom to wake him up. I started screaming, 'no this can't be! Not my baby!' He got up and was in shock also. He was like what happened. I said I found him like this in his crib. So, he called the ambulance.

When they got there, I told them how I found him and that I had fed him at about 3am that morning and put him back to sleep. They were asking me all kinds of questions even when the police got there, they started questioning the both of us as if we had done something wrong. I was not in the mood for all of that. I just wanted to know what happened to him. My neighbor came over to make sure everything was ok, and I told her what happened, and I just started crying.

The next day there was a knock at my door, it was a Pastor. He came by to talk to us about what happened and to encourage us. At the end of our conversation with him, he asked if we belonged to a church and we said no, so he invited us to his church and gave us a card with the address on it. I was not ready to speak or acknowledge God because I wanted to know why? What did I do to deserve this? It was like something in me broke.

I kept telling myself that I was not a good parent and that I didn't deserve any kids. I was so depressed after my son's passing that I barely got up to feed the kids. At night I would hear a baby crying, and I would get up and go in the room to see if he was there, but he wasn't. The pain was unbearable and on top of that I was left to grieve alone. He was not there so that we could console each other. He was out doing his thing while I was home hurting and thinking about suicide. There were so many things going on in my head. I have carried the hurt and pain of his death for years. It hurts to even sit here and write about it. But God!

As the months went by, I was still trying to pull myself together. I was losing weight, my hair was falling out, and on top of that I was about to be put out of my place. I told him about how much I needed to pay for the rent, so he told me to let him flip my money and we'd have more than enough to pay the rent. Lord, why did I do that? He took the money and 'flipped it'.

When he got home that night, I asked him where the money was and he said don't worry about it I got it, so I asked him again and he cursed at me and told me don't worry about it. I then proceeded to say some choice words back to him and the next thing I knew we were fighting.

He grabbed me and threw me on the bed and put his knees on my arms with all his weight and was trying to shove a condom in my mouth. I couldn't do anything but turn my head from left to right and try to wiggle my way out. It's like he had changed into another person. He was very angry because I kept asking about the money. He did finally get off me after I bit his finger. I was so scared to get off the bed. The only thing I could do was bawl up and cry and tell God to take me, I just wanted out.

I went through a lot in those seven years. When I look back over everything that I went through, I can say that God had his hands on me. I thank God for keeping me and my children. He brought me out of that situation and turned my life around. My self-esteem was low, my thinking was stinking, and above all things, I was broken. He had to work a miracle on me. I had to allow God to revive, reboot, and renew me. Everything was a process. No one said that it was going to be a quick fix.

BIO

I was born in Wilmington, N.C. I am the oldest of two sisters. I am the mother of five awesome children. Brittany, Shakira, Michael, Kevin and Joshua. I am also the proud grandparent to ten grandchildren. Taylor, Takari, Jada, Jaden, Cayden Callie, Caiylen, Cameron, Blue and Kyrie.

I work full time as a sales associate. While working full time I earned my Associates Degree in Biblical Studies from Safe Haven Interdenominational Bible College and Training Institute. I am currently working on my Diploma for a Pharmacy Technician.

I attend Greater Word of Truth in Garner N.C. under the leadership of Dr Apostle Freida Henderson. In October of 2018, I did my initial sermon. I am also in the dance ministry.
I believe in staying busy for the Kingdom of God.

I believe in encouraging others. I believe that God is in control no matter the outcome.
He knows all and sees all. The only thing we have to do is trust, believe,
stand on His word and hold onto the promises.

CHAPTER 4

From Pillar to Post to the Pulpit

By

Sacagawea Bunting

> And I will restore to you the years that the locust hath eaten, the cankerworm, and the caterpillar, and the palmerworm, my great army which I sent among you.
> Joel 2:25

My journey began in January 2007. I recall sitting at Union Point Park one beautiful morning when suddenly the words of the Lord calmly spoke to me saying, "Get away from your kindred to a land I will show you!" That evening I discussed the matter with my husband, and the Lord directed us to relocate to Raleigh, NC.

We immediately started packing, searching for jobs and housing. Since the school year was not over, we decided to leave our two young daughters with their grandparents. This was one of the hardest things I had ever done. At the beginning of February, we got our tax money and we both landed jobs, so we went ahead with the move.

We loaded the truck, kissed our babies goodbye, and started on our new journey. I was both nervous and excited. Growing up in a small town, everybody was either family or knew everybody. Besides, I had never ever been away from my family. We stayed with my sister until we found a place of our own.

Finally, it was the end of the school year, and the kids joined us. Shortly after we moved to a place of our own, life was good. Suddenly things changed at my job, and I went from the day shift to the overnight shift. This posed a tremendous problem since my husband worked overnight as well, so we had no one to watch the kids and I had no other choice but to quit my job.

Meanwhile, my husband was still employed but his job was going through financial issues which affected his pay. We had spent all our savings and the rent became past due. One Friday afternoon, we talked with the property owner about our situation and made a payment toward our past due account and she agreed to work with us. We breathed a sigh of relief. On that Monday, however, the property manager had a different story.

She informed us she could not accept our payment because they wanted possession of the property, and we were being evicted so she handed the money order back to us. I began to question God. Lord, what is going on, what am I going to do?

So, at once we began to get boxes and pack up our things and put them in storage. We were forced to move back to my sister's house. This was the beginning of my journey from Pillar to Post to the Pulpit. How devastating! The kids were just starting to get used to the neighborhood and making friends. This was just so unfair – everything was being ripped away.

Back at my sister's house, things were a little tense. It got so bad I sent the kids back to their grandmother's. My husband moved out and was reduced to sleeping in his car or on the couch of a couple of ole crack addicts from the neighborhood we moved from. After work I came home and stayed upstairs in the room. I did not like what was happening to my family. Just before we left our apartment complex, my husband met a young man while in the neighborhood who invited him to visit his church.

We were praying to find a church home, so we promised to attend the next Sunday. That Sunday we visited the church, everyone made us feel right at home. It was like an answer to our prayers. While at the service, the Pastor spoke life to our situation. She prophesied that my husband would get a better job and we would move into our own place. Within a couple of weeks, my husband got a better job, and we moved into our own place just like she said. It was small but cozy – most importantly, it was a place I could call my own.

Things were finally looking up. It was during this time in my life that I developed an intimate personal relationship with God. My faith began to grow, and I began to spend hours and hours in prayer. I began to be in tune with the Spirit of God and find out who I was in Christ. I decided to go to college to pursue my dream of becoming a social worker, so I quit my job in February 2009 and enrolled at the community college in the Associates of Arts program full-time.

Then, something happened that transformed my life: God called me into ministry. He gave me a new name. On March 1, 2009, I preached my initial sermon and I became an ordained minister. That same weekend, I moved into a bigger home. It was a lease to own in a quiet subdivision. The kids had their own rooms, a huge front and backyard, new schools, and new friends. We were well on our way to living the American dream. Life was good but it was short-lived.

About a year into the lease, the bank started sending letters addressed to the homeowners about foreclosure of the property. We tried contacting our property owner to no avail. Meanwhile, we continued to stay there for about six months. The foreclosure notifications continued to come. We finally decided it was time to move before the bank took possession of the property and kicked us out on the streets with nowhere to go.

We found a mobile home for rent in a nearby mobile home park. We began a new journey. I started attending college that spring and the children were now attending new schools on top of adjusting to the neighborhood and making new friends. During the next year, my husband and I became a part of the evangelism team. We meet a group of people who were living in the woods. We began ministering to them and supplying food, clothing, and toiletries.

One cold winter's night, two of the homeless men stopped by my house; they had recently moved in a wooded area in their tent near our home. I felt so bad, I called my husband in the bedroom and we both looked at each other and said, "It is too cold to let them stay in the cold," so we took the young men in. Over the next few months, the guys were staying with my family and I until the end of our lease when we went month-to-month, got behind on the rent, and were facing another eviction.

Instead, we opted to move out voluntarily. We found a condominium on the other side of town. Things were going ok until my husband got a letter that the IRS had garnished his wages. Things were already a little tight because at the time, we had more bills than money. To top it off, our Ford Expedition got repossessed. Things could not get any worse, oh, but they did. There were times we did not know where the next meal was coming from. I recall times when God would use my grandmother to be a blessing to me not even knowing my situation, she would pack my car full of food and toiletry items to take back home on my visits. She would even fill my gas tank and give me the holy ghost handshake. He also used others to bless my life.

In 2013, we got evicted for the second time from our condominium after the property owner agreed to collaborate with us. How was I going to explain this to my children? This could not be real life! I had failed as a mother. For the second time, I found myself going from Pillar to Post to the Pulpit. I did not want anyone to know what was going on, especially my family back home so I pretended everything was fine. I would brief the kids anytime we went back home or talked to family on the phone.

When we visited, I would always make sure we looked the part, so no one knew what was going on. So, we put our furniture in storage and moved in with a friend who had a family of four in their two-bedroom apartment for three or four months. Since things were cramped, my oldest daughter stayed with her best friend. During this time, we lost all our possessions in storage. I was at the lowest of lows. I had hit rock bottom. I began to stand on the word of God. I began speaking life concerning my situation. God began to turn things around. I was promoted to Elder on July 11, 2014.

You see, even though my situation had not physically changed my mindset had changed. I began to realize that what I was going through was bigger than me. Yes, my family and I were homeless, but we were learning like The Apostle Paul to be content in the state that we found ourselves in. We learned to be grateful for not just material things but for His provision, for life, health, family, and extended family. We finally got accepted into a program for homeless families. The program allowed us to stay in a single-family apartment rent-free. The requirements were that we could stay in the apartment for about ninety days, all expenses paid.

We had to attend weekly workshops, abide by a nine o'clock nightly curfew unless working, and we had to put money in an escrow account to save for housing. Even the kids attended workshops and activities that taught them about finances. At the end of the program, we graduated, and our case worker helped us find housing. She even provided us with many household items. We continued to receive case management for a year. We continued to be a blessing by allowing a couple of friends to move in.

Approximately six months went by, and we found ourselves in the same downhill spiral – we got evicted again. I thought this would never happen again, but it did. This time it lasted about two years due to the past evictions. We spent months staying in motels and extended stays until we could no longer afford it. I recall one chilly night, my husband and I spent the night in my car in the parking lot of our church because we were too prideful to ask for money. For a while we stayed with my oldest daughter and her friends until their lease was up.

We found another place to stay and then our hopes were scattered, we were told someone else had already moved in. We were right back to square one, nowhere to go. I found myself in the same cycle again, from Pillar to Post to the Pulpit. I felt broken, alone, and confused. I wanted to give up and throw in the towel. I contemplated going back to my hometown at least a dozen times, but that would admit defeat and I refused to be defeated. I am grateful for the people God placed in my life to lift me up when I was down.

At the time, I was a teacher at the academy. God used the children to lift my spirit those times when I was down. If I could not do it for myself, I had to push through for them. They were depending on me to make it, when you are going through it you better have people that will have your back and stand in the gap for you. I am thankful for my spiritual mother, Apostle Dr. Freida Henderson who not only prayed for me but encouraged me not to give up.

She told me, "Your condition is not your conclusion and where you are now is not where you are going to be." I continued to persevere despite what I was going through by leading praise and worship teaching the children at the church's K-12 academy, overseeing the brown bag ministry and nursing home ministry. I never stopped tithing and sowing seeds.

I also gave to others out of my own need. I refused to give up. That same month I was accepted for a housing program that I had applied for before. Not only did I get approved, but they paid my deposit and first month's rent. In July 2016 we got the keys to our new place. Again, we had lost all our furniture in storage, so I had to start all over from scratch. I heard the Spirit of God tell me not to get in debt to buy furniture, so I found a living room for free on Craigslist. I bought a couple of other items from a friend of a friend. A friend also gave my daughter a bed. One day I received a call from a sister asking me if I needed furniture, and I responded sure. I received a full houseful of practically new furniture.

Things were finally working out. I stayed at that apartment for about two years. After the first year, the property owner retired, and a new property manager took over. Our rent stayed the same the first year, then they decided to increase the rent, so we decided to end the lease after the next year. We moved to an upscale apartment complex. After being there about two years, my husband and I decided we no longer wanted to pay rent, it was time to own our own home. We took a leap of faith, we got boxes, and professed that we were moving. We told only a couple of people our plans. We then applied for a loan but unfortunately, we got denied. We were a little disappointed at first, but we realized that God must have a better plan. We agreed to commit to do what the realtor recommended.

On July 25, 2021, which was my forty-eighth birthday, my spiritual mother prophesied to me by shaking her keys at me and whispering I was going to get some keys. In that instance, I knew that God was up to something. Little did I know I already had the keys. In August, my grandmother who raised me from birth was unexpectedly diagnosed with pancreatic cancer which was the worst thing I had to endure. On January 2, 2022, she went home to be with the Lord, leaving me an inheritance. It was bittersweet. I come to encourage someone, no matter what you have been through or going through, there's purpose in the pain.

We do not always understand why we go through certain things, but we must trust the process. Romans 8:28 says: "And we know that all things work together for good to them that love God, to them who are called according to his purpose." If God brought you to it, He will bring you through it. This is my truth – I went from Pillar to Post to Pulpit.

Today, I am Sacagawea Bunting, Pastor of Outreach Ministries. I am a proud homeowner. He not only blessed me with a home, land, and more than I ever could ask for, think of, or ever imagine. He said He would give me double for my trouble, double for my shame. If He did it for me, He will do it for you. God is no respecter of persons. He is a promise-keeper! I give God all the glory, honor, and praise. I am thankful, even though I went through the fire I do not smell like smoke and the fire did not consume me. I won the battle because I persevered!

BIO

Please allow me to introduce myself. Hello, my name is Sacagawea Jones Bunting.
I am a native of Cove City, North Carolina. Since I was a young girl, I've always dreamed of helping others. For over 30 years, I've been working with individuals with intellectual and developmental disabilities and eldercare.

I am currently employed as a teacher assistant in the EC department at New Bern High School and direct support professional with Human Resources Unlimited. I hold an associate degree in biblical studies from Safe Haven Bible College. I was awarded Salutatorian and the Presidential Lifetime Achievement Award in 2021.

In December 2022 I was awarded support staff of the month at New Bern High School.
I've been in ministry since 2009. I serve under the leadership of Apostle Dr. Freida Henderson at Greater Word of Truth in Garner, NC.

I am inspired by my wonderful husband Louis and two beautiful daughters Taniqua and Asherah. In my leisure time I enjoy spending time with my family, reading, drawing, singing and volunteering in community outreach projects.

Dedication: I would like to dedicate this chapter to my grandmother, the late Evangelist Rosa W. Dunn for her unconditional love, prayers, teachings and demonstrating how to be a woman of faith. I love you and miss you. Continue to Rest in Peace!

SPONSORED BREAK

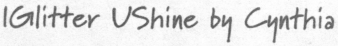

CHAPTER 5

Assignment or Attack
By
Felicia Dodson

Growing up in church from the age of 2, watching my mother serve God faithfully, is the reason I have a relationship with the Most High God today. Watching my mother pray on her knees at night and read the Bible by day, wondering who mama was talking to and what she was reading. Teaching the gospel of Jesus Christ was her mission, making it clear that God would change their lives. Watching my mother inspired me which is why I decided to get to know God and His Son Jesus for myself. I'm so glad I did because without my relationship with God there is no way I could have made it through my personal storms.

In 2014, after 20 years of marriage, I went through a painful separation and divorce even though I prayed for God to heal my marriage. I had faith He could, but I had to learn that I only have control over myself. God showed me favor through answered prayers many times, but what do you do when God says not right now, or how about flat-out no? You keep trusting Him. After my failed marriage, I decided to take time to get to know me all over again. As a woman who loved God, I was confident God had a plan for me that was good. Encouraging women to become the best version of themselves became my mission. I was a manager in corporate America and a Mary Kay consultant and in 2018 became a licensed realtor, and met a man I thought I was going to marry, spend the rest of my life with.
I was living my happily ever after, so I thought.

THE QUIET STORM

May 2019, while working out in my garage, I got bit on my leg by what I thought was a spider. It was a weird bite. Red, swollen, and a little pus to the point I went to urgent care because it looked infected. They gave me antibiotic cream to put on it and advised me if the swelling and redness wasn't gone in 48 hours to come back. It did begin to go down but a dark scar remained.

June 2019, I took a trip to Florida, to celebrate my significant other's birthday along with my nephew and his new wife. We went to theme parks, bought a timeshare, met with some friends, and just had a really good time. On the last day before heading to the airport to return home, we decided to have lunch and take a short boat trip and I became so weak in my legs and fell. I got up and began walking again, but was unable to walk far before needing to stop and rest my legs to keep from falling again.

This continued from the boat ride to the airport. I struggled walking through the airport and could not figure out what was going on. The next morning, I went to the doctor and all kinds of tests were run. The results came back: everything was fine. Even though I felt a little better, clearly there was a problem. My doctor referred me to a neurologist, and he offered physical therapy. I did therapy and seemed to feel a bit better, however over the course of the next six months, I began getting worse, experiencing heart palpitations, muscle pain like arthritis, brain fog, fatigue, shortness of breath, and headaches. My body felt like it was swollen on the inside. When I ate certain foods, I could feel the food travel through my body.

I told people it felt like food was going to my feet causing heaviness in my legs making it very difficult to walk. Of course they looked at me like I was crazy and I started to think I was crazy. I went to the doctor again and they took more tests and still could not tell me what was wrong. Test results and labs returned as normal. My body was shutting down and no one could tell me why. I went into a deep depression because none of this made any sense. I was at a place where my ability to walk became harder day by day. Getting up in the middle of the night to go to the bathroom was not an option, because I was scared that if

I got up, I would not be able to make it to the bathroom without falling, or being so weak and out of breath, I wouldn't be able to lift myself off the toilet. I could barely lift my hand or wipe my butt, because I was so weak, with no strength to truly wash my body effectively, I couldn't bend my legs to walk down the stairs so I had to slide down the steps to keep from falling. Mornings for me became more difficult daily because I had no energy in the mornings. If I could just make it downstairs and have coffee, it gave me a little energy, but coming downstairs was a chore. Falling had become my norm. All that I was going through and still no diagnosis.

My Egypt

I was in such a dark and hopeless place and I convinced myself this was my end. I just went into a state of depression. Living became so hard until I thought there was nothing else for me to do here and I wanted to die. I began to feel sorry for myself; my faith, my confidence, my praise was gone. I stayed in that state for about two months.

One morning, while lying in my bed, The Holy Spirit gave me a rude awakening and reminded me, "I am the Lord your God. I am the same God yesterday today and for evermore. The God that healed you from a herniated disc, the God that removed the tumor from your body, the God that kept your ex-husband and son out of prison when they were facing 25 years to life in prison, I'm the same God that healed your mother when she had pneumonia at the age of 87, I'm the same God that told you to go home when your daughter tried to commit suicide when you were planning to go to the grocery store on your way home from work, just to name a few of many.

I'm still here waiting to hear from you. I move in your Faith as I always have before."
All I could do was lay in my bed crying. I could not believe – I was in such a dark place. I had lost my praise, my worship, and faith without realizing it, which has always been where I got my strength and power. He told me that I have been prepared and greatly equipped for this battle and although this battle seems greater, He is still the same God. It was time to get up and fight because the battle was already won. He reminded me of the scripture that was planted inside me when I was a little girl by my mother. Proverbs 3:5-6: "Trust in the Lord Your God, with all your heart and lean not to your own understanding, but in all your ways, acknowledge me and I will direct your path."

That is exactly what He did. He told me to see and speak my healing, with the authority given to me, the same way I prayed in every other situation knowing it was already done, and that's what I did. I stopped speaking to God complaining and murmuring and began speaking to my body about my God. I declared and decreed His word over my life before getting out of my bed every morning. Reading Psalms 23, 91, 92, 93, 103 and Mark 11:22-26 each day, I began to get stronger, taking back my power, my authority, my confidence, and my faith. I watched Season 9 of Sunday Best every morning. I would lay in my bed most mornings barely able to move, so weak and in so much pain.

Then I heard the voice of God say, "Get up and praise me. Praise me in advance for your healing." It was like a one-on-one boot camp with the Lord. It wasn't easy but I obeyed, and each morning it got better. I began with a 30 second praise dance holding on to the dresser, and then over a period of time I began lifting 5 lb weights to the music and, over a 30-45 day period, began walking the treadmill. He told me to start with 3 minutes and progressively get to 30 minutes, and then walk outside. I was doing better, on the road to recovery with no diagnosis.

September 2019, I fell down 15 cement steps and was rushed to the hospital. I suffered a concussion and bruises, but no broken bones, I praised God!
This entire situation definitely challenged my faith, but I refused to let that fall discourage me. I literally had to drive back to the church where I fell, looking at those steps, and praised God for sparing my life. I know that I was truly blessed. That fall could have killed me. All I can remember saying is: "God, you definitely have a purpose for my life." Unfortunately, it got worse. October 2019, I began a new job, working part-time as a realtor.

December 2019, I was entering work and someone who was walking in front of me backed into me accidentally and knocked me down. I fell backwards, bumped my head on the concrete ground. I was rushed to the hospital. I suffered another concussion, now I had blurred vision, dizziness, headaches, and brain fog, muscle weakness, pain and fatigue, sleepless nights, and was unable to drive. During conversation, I repeated myself, losing my train of thought, forgetting what I was talking about. I was truly going through it and all I could do was cry out to the Lord for strength as I continued to pray, fast, and praise, having faith this too shall pass, and now unable to work.

My Exodus

January every year, I fast with my church. No food from 6-6 the first week of the year. January 2020, God had another plan. He instructed me to fast, with the Greater Word of Truth, led by Apostle Freida Henderson, an anointed woman of God. My sister from another mother was a member of this church. I only met the Apostle once, but I obeyed.

This fast was for 3 weeks and consisted of no meat, no sugar. Only fish, fruits, and vegetables. In 3 days, my body felt so good. Less pain, no weakness. I had so much energy, I couldn't believe it. I felt like I could run around the block. This fast changed my life. It was definitely the hand of God. At the end of the fast, I visited the church but I didn't get a chance to share my testimony with the Apostle at that time and due to the outbreak of Covid -19, everything shut down.

After the fast, I went back to eating normally and the symptoms came back fully. I went back to the doctor in February and explained how my body no longer tolerated meats and other foods without me being in pain and experiencing weakness in my body. More tests were taken. This time, the tests revealed I had flu-like symptoms, inflammation in my body, allergies to corn, shrimp, wheat, and milk. Food I had been eating all my life. I could no longer eat chicken without pain. What in the world was going on? I used to tell people God created chicken just for me. Still no diagnosis. I continued seeking God for revelation because the doctors were clueless and I was exhausted.

God's Revelation

I began my own research about inflammation and its causes, and what causes flu-like symptoms, and through my research God revealed to me I had Lyme disease. Get this, I called my doctor and told him that I have Lyme disease. Based on my symptoms, the blood work, and the bull's-eye rash on my leg, it was clear that's what I had. I learned that Lyme disease is very hard to detect and most people are bedbound for years before they find out they have it, as they normally don't understand that the food we eat plays a major role in how our body is affected.

Sugar, dairy, and gluten fed the antibodies the tick released into my body that allowed the antibodies to live in the cells of my body and caused me to become allergic to many foods that I was able to eat before. My doctor stated that Lyme disease was the only disease I was not tested for. How did I get Lyme disease? The bug bite that I got back in May 2019 while working out in the garage was a tick bite and I still had the dark bull's-eye rash on my leg.

So now finding out it had been in my system for months was devastating because I was in late-stage Lyme disease where there was not much that could be done to cure the Lyme disease because the antibiotics needed to be given within 30 days of the bite for the best results to be rid of or prevent the antibodies from the tick from taking residence in my cells. I had to rely on God to heal me, because when I called centers for help with Lyme disease, I was required to pay out-of-pocket as insurance doesn't cover treatments and the cost could be anywhere from $25,000 to $50,000.

My Healing

May 2021, watching a service online, Apostle Freida Henderson spoke these prophetic words into my life, a message from God. She said, "God can do anything; even while you are in your kitchen, God can heal you." She said, "Felicia, it's already done. First you must know the will of God in order to know when God has moved." What seemed like a disappointment was really the hand of God. She said, "God is strengthening you right now,". She said, "Stand strong in your faith and don't waiver."

What was so powerful about this word is she had no idea I was sitting in my kitchen and my mother sitting across from me, with no idea what I was going through in my health, or my broken relationship, but God did. He used this woman of God to bless my entire soul; sitting in my kitchen, with tears in my eyes, God gave me the wisdom and the strength to continue to fight in faith and showed me the diet to eat that healed both myself and my 88-year-old mother from high blood pressure and COPD. Not only was my Faith increased, but longsuffering was added to my resume. I am stronger spiritually than ever. A powerhouse for the kingdom of God. An assignment indeed. I am convinced that nothing is too hard for God.

To God be the Glory!

BIO

My name is Felicia Dodson, I am a mother of 2 children, a son and a daughter and the grandmother of 10, which both of my children delivered a set of fraternal twins. I have 2 living siblings, a sister and a brother out of 6 and my mother who is 90. I have been in Corporate America all my career and have obtained many skills and climbed the ladder from a temp to management.

I have been in church all my life. I grew up Baptist, then changed to COGIC as an adult, where I learned so much about praying, fasting and the power of God, under great leaders, which I learned to read and study the bible. I attended school to obtain an Evangelist license while teaching bible study. I became a Youth Leader, served as Pastors aid, Armor Bearer, & Missions, ministering in Women's shelter, Hospitals, and Nursing homes.

In 2008 my husband at the time, my daughter and myself moved to Raleigh NC where I continued my career, became a Mary Kay consultant, obtained my Real Estate License and obtained a Notary License. I attended a Pentecostal Freewill Baptist Church where I served in Choir, Praise Team, taught children Sunday school and a led a program for young girls called the Daisies. I was also Dean of Women at a camp for abused children that lasted for a week each year. I was a part of this camp for 6 years until my untimely illness in 2019.

Covid- 19 shut down churches in 2020 so I began to watch Greater Word of Truth online and was truly blessed. I became a member in 2021 & obtained an Associate's Degree in Biblical Studies.

In my journey I have learned that the greatest achievement in my life is my relationship with the Most High God, His Son Jesus the Christ and His Word. I am blessed to be a woman of Faith that moves mountains. The Most High God uses me to be an Intercessor Prayer for friends, family, strangers and our nation. He reveals many things to me in dreams and visions and through His word and gives divine revelations.

I can truly say, this Assignment definitely reveals the Power of God in my life as my Healer. So many things happen in our life to develop us into who God wants us to be and at the same time show His Power and Glory to all. The Most High does not want us to rely on anyone or anything but Him.

I am truly blessed to be a part of His elect to, to carry out the assignments in which He has given to me and maintain my Faith in His Son Jesus the Christ and Keeping His commandments. Reading the Bible, gaining much Wisdom, Knowledge and Understanding supersedes all the things in my life in which I thought I was living my best life were the things of the world. When you read and know who you are in the Bible, your entire life changes. I have a true love for the Most High God, and a great desire to motivate and inspire women to reach their full potential.

SPONSORED BREAK

CHAPTER 6

Abandoned But Not Forgotten

By

Tanya Holley

I could hear the shower water running and this was my chance to break away for a snack. I was instructed to sit on the couch and not move until my mother finished taking her shower. Did I listen to the instructions? Well no, because I was hungry. Therefore, I got off the couch and headed into the kitchen. As I looked around, I noticed that the snacks resided on the top of the refrigerator.

What's a kid to do to get something to eat around here, I thought to myself. So, I devised a plan to take the chair from the kitchen table and use it to get what I wanted from the top of the fridge. As I was standing on the seat it began to wobble, then suddenly, BAM! The seat had fallen straight down with me standing on top of it. To my surprise, looking at me with her towel wrapped around her was my mother. She was full of rage at this act of disobedience.

"Look what you've done, I told you not to move and you damaged my chair. I am so sick of you and your stupidity, "she said. "Now get over here." I could see that she was getting angry, it was like a lion was growling inside of her, and the roaring thunderous sound of her voice made me nervous. I wanted to obey but my body was paralyzed with fear and I could not honestly move. This act of defiance only infuriated her. "Move now. What are you, deaf? MOVE!" I could sense that this was not going to go well for me. Was it the chair, I thought to myself, or was it something else that ignited her frustration?

Since I could not answer the question or move, she grabbed me by my forearms, using a firm grip to lift me.

My body was now suspended in the air and thrown to the wall. She then said, "Get up," as she talked down to me. I did as I was gasping for air; her next choice I was not ready for. She grabbed me with such force and proceeded to repeatedly slam my body up against the wall. It felt like I was going from wall to wall.

The room was spinning and silent. I just knew that I was leaving this Earth. Just then my body collapsed to the floor, and I blacked out. I was abandoned, left on the cold floor to die. I just remember waking up in the hospital. Although I am not sure how long my hospital stay was, I do remember opening my eyes and seeing two strangers at my bedside. I began to panic and became very anxious.

I began screaming for my brother, I needed to see him and wanted to know if he too was safe. Bursting through the door came my brother with a doctor. I reached for him with arms stretched wide as he ran into them; I held on to him tightly as if to say please never leave me.

We smiled at each other and he leaned in to kiss my forehead. The doctor had good news and he told us that we were going home. Before he could say another word, I had another anxiety attack. I shouted, "Home, I don't want to go," with tears in my eyes. The doctor could not have understood the trauma that I just experienced. The older lady by my bedside placed her hand on top of mine and said, "You are coming with us." It was the calmness in her tone that captivated me, and her radiant smile controlled my anxiety. The gentleman that was beside her held my brother firmly in his arms, and they both said in unison that everything will be alright.

They were right, everything was going to be alright; we did not go back to our biological mother but stayed with them for a short while until we were placed somewhere more permanent. It would have been unsafe to place us back into an environment of abuse and neglect – I probably would not be here if that had happened – we needed an environment that provided safety and security. They provided us with that, and I am forever grateful. We were placed in foster care and stayed in the system for five years.

I was three at the initial placement and got adopted out at eight years of age. My brother and I were blessed, we were able to stay with our foster mother for five consecutive years. Never once were we uprooted, I now know that there was a greater power that was protecting us and sustaining us.

During my years in the system, nagging questions lingered in my mind. Questions like why did my mother not like me? And why was she so violent towards me? This traumatic experience caused resentment, depression, and low self-esteem that lasted for years.

Watch what you say.

The words we speak and deposit into others have a lasting effect on someone's life. You have the power to choose what your words can do and become in the atmosphere. People will always remember what you say and how that made them feel. I remember having visitation with my biological mother. I was nervous and excited at the same time. She was kind and gentle with me, but that did not last long. She went to cleanse my hair, she was pulling kind of rough, and I began to cry.

At that moment she became angry with me and shouted, "Be still," and said these words that I embodied for much of my life: "Aint nobody ever going to do anything for you or love you. So, you better learn to do it yourself." Then she walked away. I felt that to my core and held on to 'no one will love me'. For years I built up walls, not allowing people to get close to me. I would push people away intentionally and was very standoffish at times. I was emotionally awkward when it came to receiving compliments.

I resented her for saying that to me, although she may have been speaking from a broken place, it was hurtful to me. Therefore, by treating people that way I was walking in HER TRUTH, not MY TRUTH. I wanted something new, and God created in me a clean heart and a renewed a right spirit within me. (Psalm 55:10)

Factors that contributed to my low self-esteem.

For years my brother and I waited for our forever family. Five years, to be exact, and the waiting was mentally draining. During that time, each year we would go to adoption fairs. This is where the agency would host an event for families to come and provide them with an opportunity to adopt a child. You had to smile and meet different people every year, it was excruciating to attend. However, I was smiling on the outside but hurting on the inside.

Understand that my childhood of being abused and living in foster care molded my self-esteem. I had rehearsed what my mother told me, therefore, I felt unlovable. It also did not help with the adoption fairs where people get to pick and choose who they wanted to take home. I suffered immensely internally as we waited and waited for a family to love us.

I overheard a conversation once in passing where they would say things like: "I like the girl, but we don't want the boy," or they would say, "We already have a girl, we don't want her, she is too old, we want someone younger," or vice versa. For years I thought that we were never going to get adopted; we were undesirable, unloved, and forgotten. Once again, the angels that were looking out for us before were at work again. What seemed like and felt like no one wanted us, was turned in our favor. In 1983, my brother and I were adopted. We went with our forever family.

FEAR!

This new transition in my life took some time. I was in a new environment and I feared the unknown, not knowing what my future held with this family. I could not enjoy anything because of my overthinking. I would think, what if I was not a good kid, would they send us back? And most importantly, would I be loved? I had this warped image of what this family life would be. It took me a long time to call them mom or dad, so I settled on calling them Mr. and Mrs. This was my comfort level in the beginning, and then about a year or so later I felt comfortable calling them mom and dad. Is this normal you might ask; I am not sure, but for me, I needed to feel safe, and waiting made it make sense to me.

I have to say that this family was fun. We were enrolled in gymnastics, swimming, dance, and modeling, just to name a few activities. Whatever their biological children participated in we too were included. One would be excited, but I was afraid. Some may call me a scaredy cat, but it was fear that I was entangled with. Let me just clarify that fear is a normal part of life, it is part of our nervous system and it gives us our survival instinct.

However, for me, my fear was unhealthy because it made me more cautious of who was watching and what people had to say every waking moment of my life. Sadly, I always operated on this level of fear. I would make excuses for not trying. I gave fear permission to suffocate my potential and rob me of happiness. I wanted to be happy, and I wanted to walk in God's per-fect will.

I knew that God has a plan for my life and that his plans do not include fear. God did not give us a spirit of fear but of power, love, and a sound mind (2nd Timothy 1:7). I wanted a sound mind; I was so tired of wrestling with fear. I knew that I could not reach my potential by living in fear. Since I have been transformed, I do not operate in fear. I now encourage others not to let fear suffocate their potential, but to always believe in themselves.

The revolving door of abuse.

Let's fast forward to my adult years, I am now in my early twenties and I met someone I was in love with. This was not a good connection, as you can gather from the title of this section of the story. I ended up in something that was not good for me. I wanted this love because everyone I knew was in love and I wanted what they had. They seemed to be so happy, so I thought. I was excited and overjoyed but had no idea what I was getting myself into. The beginning stage was fun until it went to Hell in a handbasket.

I found myself playing house and doing wifey things, but to him, I was just a friend, no title. You know the different titles you get when they are cheating on you. You are either their roommate, cousin, or friend – I digress. I made the relationship comfortable for him to disrespect me. So why should I say anything now, what gave me the right to now change my mind on how things were going?

He wasn't threatened by me; I was a joke, a spineless person who would never stand up for herself. I was tired and enough was enough. I heard a conversation between him and his friend, about how he was looking for a job, but could not find one. Indeed, he needed one because my body was weary from working two and three jobs to make ends meet.

On that day I had my chance to say something. I said, "You need to look for a job or your butt is grass." I had a firm tone but was joking. I used the other word for a butt that rhymes with grass. As I began to walk away, I glanced at his face and noticed his facial expression change in an instant. It went from a chuckle to hatred. He felt humiliated in front of his company and I was going to pay for that insult, that joke turned into a domestic violence assault.

Not again, I thought, as he caught me in the bedroom with a hook here and there. I ran out of the bedroom fleeing for my life. I took my keys and out the front door I went. I was chanting to myself, "Go, Tanya, go," and just like a defensive lineman tackles a quarterback, I went down to the ground. He was on top of me pounding me in my head and punching me in my temple. Sure, this sounds horrific, but it was the punch to my temple that triggered something in me to fight back. Somehow, the light bulb of justice came on. A supernatural power came over me. The little girl inside of me was fighting for ME.

I was kicking, screaming, scratching, and punching. I felt empowered! To be honest I was imagining all the wrong that was done to me as a child. I managed to break free and get to my car and leave. I was a nervous wreck and everyone I needed was nowhere to be found. I sat in the park and cried out to the Lord for help. Yes, I was in a backslidden state, but I knew to call on the name of the Lord for help.

When I came back to my apartment the door was ajar, and when I peeped my head inside, he was nowhere to be found. I was nervous to go inside but what I witnessed next was a nightmare. Everything that I owned was destroyed, things were broken and slashed, but I was alive. I had the sense to call His name, and the word tells us Call unto me, and I will answer thee, and show the great and mighty things, in which thou knowest not (Jeremiah 33:3).

Breaking the cycle and becoming Resilient!

I may have been forgotten by my biological mother but not by God. God had equipped me with the fortitude to face my adversity with a positive attitude and the capacity to bounce back. I am here to tell someone who is reading this story, that in every trial, test, heartache, and setback there is a purpose for it. When those memories of the past arise, pull on your inner strength to push past them. You are stronger than you think and that, my dear reader, is called resilient. Trust the process!

BIO

Author Tanya Holley was born and raised in Brooklyn, New York. Her family moved to Sarasota, Florida when she was twelve years old, this is where she calls home because all her family lives there. Back in 2001 in need to change her environment she moved to Raleigh, NC, back in 2017 she left the city and moved to the countryside of Willow Spring, NC.

For the past nine years, Tanya has worked full time for Wake Public County Schools System as an instructional assistant. While working full time back in 2008 she graduated from Shaw University with a bachelor's degree in Liberal Arts, and now she is pursuing her Associate degree in Early Childhood education from Wake Tech University.

Tanya is a member of Greater Word of Truth in Garner, NC under the leadership of Apostle Dr. Freida Henderson. In February 2016 she preached her initial sermon and came forth as an evangelist of the gospel, where she serves on evangelism ministry and on the usher ministry as head usher.

Tanya loves to encourage others and love to see everyone around her win in life. She loves to read and study God's word which enriches her soul daily to be equipped to minister to others. She has many scriptures but with the busyness of life, her favorite scripture is Psalm 46:10 which is "Be still and know that I am God: I will exalted among the heathens, I will be exalted in the earth."

SPONSORED BREAK

CHAPTER 7

Trusting God Through Tragedy & Pain

By
Brenda Barkley

Have you ever had something so detrimental happen in your life that it could only make you rise from it? You could only rise from it because folding in on yourself was not an option.

Where do I start? I guess that I will just get to the point. In the summer of 2019, September 8th to be exact, my life changed dramatically. My kids and I were attacked, and we almost died at the hands of the one person who was supposed to always protect us: my husband, their father.

Though this is difficult to talk about, I am being healed. This is a process that isn't even for me, but for someone else out there who might have been through the same tragedy, something similar, or domestic abuse, who can't bring themselves to speak about it. Therefore, the hurt that they are feeling, the sorrow, the pain, the anger, the disappointment, will not go away so the healing cannot begin.

It took me this long to come to terms with what really happened, even to this day it seems hard to believe. People see the outside of you and think that you are okay, but on the inside, you are torn, devastated, and we carry this with us every day. We all can put up a big front for people to see what we want them to see because if they really see what's going on inside of us, we can't handle it.

I was devastated. Period. I had been with this man for 27 years and married to him for 25 years at that time. Though everything hadn't always been peaches and cream (so to speak), I would have never thought that he would do anything this detrimental. Or did I? 'Im just speaking my truth.

When I married in 1995, I asked God to only let me have desire for my husband and no other man and He fulfilled that promise. In our earlier years of marriage, this man took me through a lot. A LOT! Physical, mental, and emotional abuse was my life for many years, although he didn't display any of those characteristics at the start of our relationship. Abuse was my life. I kept it a secret for years, yet my kids knew. Many times, they were even a witness to it. They didn'tunderstand what was happening until they got older and understood what was happening to mommy wasn't right. To people shocked, this went on up until around the last 9 years of my marriage, when he gave his life to God.

He was an armor-bearer in the church, a deacon, and on the security team. So, I believed that everything was finally on the right track with us, in the natural and spiritual. I believed that we were in one accord. So how did we get 'here'?
I started seeing a change in him for months leading up until this incident. Though the physical abuse had no longer existed, he slowly started again with the verbal abuse. I noticed the people that he tried to help were not the people he needed to have in his life.

He reconnected with people in and of his old way of life. Let me go into a little bit of his old way of life, before he gave his life to Christ. He was a city boy from up north and I was a country girl that was raised in the church, naive to a lot of worldly things. When I met him, unbeknownst to me, he was a drug dealer that had connections with high-ranking drug dealers. Not only was he selling, but I found out that he was also using. Crack and cocaine were his choice of drugs. By the time I found out, I was already in love, and we had been together for two years. Soon after, I found myself pregnant with what would be our first child, out of three together. We got married and had our firstborn.

There were times when I would wake up in the middle of the night and my husband would be gone on one of his several drug-runs and drug binges. I don't know why he even sold drugs because he gave away more things than what he sold (how does that work?). I can't take from him that he had a good heart and would help anyone he could. I saw him give his last many times, even taking from his family because someone was in need. That was one of the characteristics that made me fall in love with him, but the addiction had a hold of him at this point. I just didn't know the magnitude of it yet.

A lot of times, I ignored it and prayed to God that it would get better because when we made vows to God, I planned on keeping those vows forever. We had small kids and I wanted them to grow up in a two-parent home because I didn't have that growing up. So, I endured that life. But my God will provide a way of escape even when we don't know that's what we need.

The tragic incident took place on a Sunday, some of the details I cannot remember, or I guess I blocked it from my mind. I recall that we had come from church, and I got on my husband for being disrespectful to me and how he made us look because of some of the decisions that he made. But he always believed that his decisions were always right and if he felt like doing something, whether you agreed or not, then he was going to do it.

Very seldomly would he compromise. We argued and my youngest daughter was on my side; he didn' tlike that. My son had gone outside in the backyard and my husband became even more angry, using profanity, words that I never want to repeat. He was in my face and at that point our oldest daughter came home, heard us arguing, and got me to come into her room. He then went to the backyard, and we could hear him screaming at my son. He proceeded to bring my son back inside the house, irate.

At this point, he called us all into the living room. He said something concerning my son, but I can' t recall what. My oldest daughter and I were trying to calm everything down at that point. Our youngest daughter had her phone and he asked her if she was recording him. She didn' t reply but kept holding her phone. That really took him over the edge. It was like something in him snapped and he flew into a rage.

We watched him walk away so we thought it was over. When we were on our way outside, he came back in the living room and went towards my youngest daughter. He raised his hand and we then noticed it was a butcher knife that he had in his hand. We were all screaming at this point, telling him to stop, grabbing him everywhere we could.

It was like he had the strength of Superman. He was swinging the knife, stabbing her repeatedly. My son later told me that he saw a tall black figure over my husband. Later when I told my pastor this, she said it was a demon. When God brings you out of something and has brought you through it, you don' t go back to what He has brought you through!

My youngest daughter stumbled out the front door as he then turned his rage on me. He began stabbing me as my youngest son and I were trying to make our way out the backdoor. We pleaded for him to stop, fighting for our lives. He only relented when our oldest daughter ran into the kitchen to retrieve a knife. He was after her now and stabbed her multiple times before she was able to flee. His rage was not over though. I don' t know how the backdoor came open since there was a stick behind the sliding door to prevent us from getting out. It could only have been God!

As I was running in the backyard, I tripped and fell. I pleaded with him to stop as he was repeatedly stabbing me. My son heard and came after him, hitting him in the head. He stabbed my son again. My son ran behind the shed, and it was like my husband froze and went back inside the home. We all met up, except for my youngest daughter; I couldn' t find her. Unbeknownst to us, she had run to a neighbor' s house for help.

We saw him come to the front door as we were fleeing, but he didn' t come after us again. We ran across the street to our neighbor' s house, frantically knocking on the door. They peeped out the peephole and looked through the blinds, but still, they didn' t open the door. So we kept running and we don' t know why we stopped at this particular neighbor' s house.

We found ourselves banging on the door. A lady opened the door for us. She told us that she doesn'tknow why she opened the door because she never opens the door for anyone, especially late in the evening. I knew it was God Almighty!

When she saw the condition that we were in, she made us sit down. Her and her two daughters proceeded to wrap towels around our wounds as best they could to stop the blood flow. I remember my daughter asked me, "Mom, are we going to die?" She said, "Mommy, I don't want to die." I looked at her and said, "Baby, we are not going to die. God got us." all the time praying "God, please let my children be okay." The lady's daughters began speaking life over my kids, encouraging them with the Word of God. It was at a point when I wondered why our first neighbor didn't open the door for us.

Then the Holy Spirit said to me, "It was the second house that God knew that His word would be spoken into you all. There was a language barrier at the first house that you ran to, and they wouldn't have been able to do that." The ambulance was called. It was a while before they got to us because multiple calls had been made from different people. We didn't realize that the house my youngest daughter ran to was calling 911 also.

The police had to shut off all routes to us to secure the perimeter in case my husband was still near the area. Once secured and they found that the threat was gone, the ambulance was allowed to proceed on route to us. All of us were taken to the hospital in different ambulances. Imagine being a parent in the hospital, fighting for your life, knowing your kids were also fighting for their lives but not being able to get to them.

From the stabbing, my youngest son's, youngest daughter's, and my lungs were punctured. We had to have blood transfusions and surgery was performed to put chest tubes inside to drain fluid from our lungs. I was hooked up to IVs on both sides of me. Our oldest daughter received multiple stab wounds but got treated and thank God she was able to go home!

My pastor was there for hours while they stabilized us, never leaving. When she finally was able to see me, she didn't even say a word. She just looked at me and shook her head. She held my hand, and I was able to draw strength just from her presence. I would later tell her that the Bible says, "The prayers of a righteous man availeth much."

Sometimes people say things when they are angry and don't mean it. I know from experience that has been me. I have said things when I was mad that I didn't mean and never would have done, but that's why you have to be careful about what you speak in the atmosphere.
The tongue has the power of life and death (Proverbs 18:21).
You can speak things into existence.

en you speak things into the atmosphere, remember that Satan hears you as well as God.
v this one thing: Satan is not going to act on it in a positive way as God would, but in a
eyative way. The stakes are high. Our tongues can build others up or they can simply tear
them down. One thing my husband would always say was "Man can't kill me because I'm
already dead." I would ask him, "What does that even mean?" "Stop speaking that into the
atmosphere."

A few months before this incident happened, he had acquired some land and a home that he
didn't have to pay for. I gave the testimony one Tuesday night at Bible study about how God
had blessed us. My pastor told our testimony during one Sunday morning service and I
remember her saying to him that, "Your wife, Evangelist Brenda [my title at the time], she's
your favor." He smiled during the service, but when we got home, he let me know that he was
not pleased about her saying that. That was just another indication that something was going on
with him that wasn't of God.

I remember my pastor said to the ministers one day that our initial sermon would be our
testimony. She asked me about the title of my initial sermon. I told her my title was "To Be
Covered by The Blood." Little did I know that I would be tried by my initial sermon, but if it
hadn't been for the blood that Jesus shed, when he hung, bled, and died on Calvary cross,
we wouldn't have made it. The blood of Jesus kept us. I dare not give up on God!

I serve the devil notice today that he can't have my joy, my peace, my breakthrough, my family,
and he can't have me! I'm serving him notice that what he thought for our bad, God turned it
around for our good! Somebody asked me how I could go on after this. I said, "Because I will not
let this determine how I live the rest of my life. I will not let it dictate my destiny or have the
power over me to keep me bound in that situation."

God knows through me not giving up that he can trust me, and I know that I can trust God.
I have a shirt that says, "The Devil whispered in my ear: you are not strong enough to withstand
the storm. Today I whispered in the devil's ear. I am a child of God, a woman of faith,
A WARRIOR OF CHRIST, I am the storm." I'm not the victim. I'm an overcomer!

BIO

Elder Brenda Barkley, known to family as Necey, was born in Franklinton, North Carolina to the parents of Willie James Johnson and deceased mother Catherine Dunston. Being raised by a devout Christian mother, Brenda gave her life to God at a young age.

Brenda was one of four children between Willie and Catherine. She came from humble beginnings but was surrounded by love. Brenda came from a family of singers. So, from a young age she sung in a quartet group for over 30 years. It was one of the greatest joys of her life being able to minister with song.

Brenda is blessed with five children Kariya, Trai, Adonnas, Aaliyah, and Aaron. She is the grandmother of five grandchildren, two boys (Jacob and Nicolas), and three girls (Kamari, Zariya, and Makayla). On October 18th, 2018, she preached her initial sermon. The title of the sermon was To Be Covered by The Blood. Little did she know that less than a year later, the title of her sermon would be her testimony!

She was later ordained an elder under the leadership of her pastor, Apostle Dr. Freida Henderson. She is an active member of Greater Word of Truth in Garner, NC under Apostle Dr. Freida Henderson. In her free time, Brenda enjoys being with loved ones, singing, reading, and to anyone that knows her, being a comedian. She currently resides in Raleigh, NC for the past 30 plus years.

Despite the many struggles that she has faced, she pressed on to pursue and obtain her associate degree in Biblical Studies. This gave her the push to also pursue and obtain her bachelor's degree in Biblical Studies. She knew she needed to press her way because someone needed to know how she made it through. She had to shed many tears, endured through great pain, loss, and sorrow, but she always reached back and pulled from Psalm 23. Her philosophy is, no matter what comes her way, with God she always WINS!

CHAPTER 8
Burden To Blessing
By
Stephanie Carter

I believe that the Superwoman Complex was born out of imitation and/or necessity.
My entire life has been about being a caregiver and going the extra mile for others.
On this Christian journey, I have learned to overcome the Superwoman complex and use
it to benefit the Kingdom of God.

Superwomen step up to do what needs to be done in the absence of a competent male figure.
The education of the superwoman sometimes begins at a young age. We are taught by our
struggling single mothers. For most of my childhood, my mother was single. She educated me
as to what a mother has to do in order to provide for her children. She worked as many as 2
full-time jobs and 2 special holiday jobs (Christmas, Thanksgiving, and back to school).
As her role changed, so did mine. Necessity demanded a role
change; therefore, I had to step up and become whatever
my mother and family needed.

The problem with being a superwoman is the following:
1- she is strong, and 2- she requires no help. When one
adopts this behavior, it is perceived that she needs no
assistance and thus she does not get any.
Superman requires nothing and he is strong.
Once it is established that a superwoman can do it
alone then she will always be left to get the job done alone.

I remember, as a child of 13 years (or so)
my grandmother sat me down and began having
a serious conversation. She sat directly in front of
me and held both of my hands. She said,
"You are the oldest. Everyone is watching you.
You are to be an example for the others
(brothers and sisters)." I thought about it
and said to her, "I don't care.
I'm just a kid and I want to have fun too."

She said "You can't. You have to be responsible. It is your job as the oldest to teach the other children to do right. You have to be their role model." I went from helping out to becoming a substitute mother, babysitter, cook, tutor, and/or whatever was needed. What I did to assist her became my responsibility, my burden.

I remember as a young adult, my youngest sister and I were having an argument. She was complaining that she received less attention and I received more. It was at that time that I realized that I always defaulted my needs to those of my brothers and sisters. We were a family of 5 children. I always placed their needs above my own. The position of being the oldest has always placed more responsibility on that child. I was no exception. The grooming of the superwoman continues.

One day as a young adult, I kept having a recurring dream. I saw myself as a small girl approximately 7 years of age. I was standing at a grave site. I stood between my mother on my right and a smaller boy on the left, holding hands. I asked her what it meant because it was always a fuzzy picture. She said, "I can'tbelieve you remembered that. That was so long ago. That was at your baby brother's grave site. You held my hand the entire time." Thus beginning my career as a caregiver. I believe caregiving was ingrained at this early age as a need to help my mother and brother through this sad occasion.

I married in 1983, and all was well until it wasn't. In 1980, my husband was admitted into a drug rehabilitation program. He missed so many days of work until he was dismissed. He would steal all of my paycheck (it was a race to the bank on payday) and he would withdraw his entire paycheck and spend it all until his return home 1 to 3 days later. I had to take things into my own hands. I hid my checkbook and only used the card. This worked well because he never knew my PIN number.

There would be times that my son and I would eat at a co-worker's house because we had no food. There were times that we had no running water or electricity because I had no money to pay the bills. This superwoman wrote a bad check to turn the utilities back on, then paid penalty charges to the bank. I had to do what I had to do.

This superwoman had to make a huge decision. To remain in a marriage that taught our son that a good woman stays regardless of the situation did not work in my mind. This good wife worked and went to school full-time and the dad took a child to a drug house, which made me ultimately leave him. I realized that I was totally unable to feed our son and provide for him as long as I stayed with his dad. I just could not do to him what he was doing to us. If I cooked food, I could not deny any of it from him.

My upbringing would not allow it. That spirit of addiction was not a spirit that I was accustomed to. I could not handle his emotions and sometimes fear for my safety would cross my mind. When my husband told me that the spirit of his drug would talk to him, I knew that my husband was no longer himself. That demon had a stronghold on him that could not be challenged and my husband had zero determination to make a change.

At that time, I joined the local church and shortly thereafter had a counseling session with the pastor and his wife. We were told that sometimes someone has to make a tough decision, in order to reset the marriage. I separated from him in 1990 and finally divorced around 2006 (or so). The Bible states that God won't give you more than you can bear. Those years brought me to a place of prayer and fasting for my husband's deliverance.

In 1994, after giving birth to my middle son, I was on a diet in order to lose my pregnancy weight. As I was losing weight, I noticed that I continued to lose weight after I got to the desired size. I would eat and eat all the time. I also noticed I was sweating profusely, having tremors, hair loss, severe dry skin, and heart palpitations. My mood swings were ridiculous – I was easily angered. I felt that I was mentally unstable and had a session with a mental health provider. I was then medically diagnosed with hyperthyroidism or Graves Disease.

After years of treatment/medication/testing, it was stabilized. Throughout my treatment I never thought to ask, "Why me?". My question was, "How did it happen?". I never learned what predisposed me to get this disorder. Later, after I was speaking with a relative, I realized that if I had not had the condition I would not have been able to connect her vague symptoms. As a result, I have been able to help multiple family members with the same disorder. My pain was not for me but to serve others. My family continues to use my testimony to help others also.

In 2001, I decided that I could open my home to other children in need. I became licensed as a foster care parent and opened my home to 2 boys. I felt that others could benefit from what I had to offer. By 2004, I had a total of 5 children that had benefited from my service. I finally adopted 3 of the children that I had cared for. My God has given me the ability to help others. My God continued to give me strength. My God kept me. My God shielded me. My God, I was exhausted.

Later in 2005, I was diagnosed with breast cancer. Even though I was a medical professional, I was devastated. Being told that I had cancer was an emotional death sentence, but I was not able to have any emotions. I had learned to care for others and not myself. I had to work full-time and maintain my parental duties because there was no one else. I didn't have time to have an emotional breakdown. What I did have was emotional numbness. I took my medications, went to radiation therapy for 14 weeks, worked full-time, and maintained the house and hildcare – I had no clarity. I just motioned through life as a zombie.

At that time, I joined Greater Word of Truth (Formerly Faith Assembly Christian Center). I was met with so much agape love and the love of Christ that I broke down. I had a conversation with the pastor and told her my issue. It was the only time that I had to express myself without depressing others. People often think they are helping but they continue to make one feel sick. Get well cards, they mean you are sick. I never wanted to feel sick or broken by my multiple surgeries and radiation.

Heaven forbid, a caregiver should need care. I only allowed my mother to help me for 2 weeks then I took back over. Once again, if it had not been for Jesus, I don't know where I would be. Because of His love, protection, healing power, and mind regulation, I don't think I would have made it. Once again, if I hadn't had that experience, I would not be able to help others. To this day, I have persons struggling through cancer treatment who I counsel, give advice, pray with, and just listen to. The love of the Lord and a kind ear can be a blessing.

My testimony has opened doors for me and others. I truly believe that if it had not been for Jesus' healing me through His 39 stripes I would have been lost to my conditions. While at a Women's Health conference, I was told that I did not look like what I had gone through. God's love had touched my face and body so that when I would tell my story, it would not bring others to fear, for God so loved us that He gave His only begotten son. My health, past and future, remains the good report of the Lord. I shall live and not die.

In 2012, my middle sister died while living with me. She went into cardiac arrest while parked in front of my house in the ambulance. They took her to the local hospital and escorted us into the family waiting area. I called my Apostle to let her know what was happening and she showed up at the hospital to help me and my family. I told her, "It is never good news when they take you to the back." God brought the Apostle – the angel – into my life for such a time as that. She brought calming assurance and love into the room at the announcement of my sister's death.

I can never thank her enough for her presence and kindness during that time. My mother and sister had difficulty regaining their composure but I had to be strong. With my nursing training, I had to hold onto my emotions in order to fully comprehend as the medical professionals began to talk about the incident. I recognized that I had to focus on what they would say regarding her death. I knew my mother would have difficulty because losing a child is devastating to a parent. Even then the Lord gave me immediate peace to calm myself so that understanding could take place. The Lord provides you with all that you need when you need it, you only need to be open to receive it.

Someone once said, "You are always the strong one. You don't need help." I retorted, "I thought you knew me. I need it more than most. I am not given the opportunity to show much emotion."

Whenever others are emotional someone has to be ever-diligent, observant, on duty, and clear-headed. There has got to be some downtime. Even the great oak breaks from constant bending and bowing. My God hears me, keeps me, and sustains me. His grace and mercy endure forever. And then it came to me. It was ordained that I be born first because the others would not be able to handle the pressure.

When my mother encouraged me to go to nursing school, I completed it. My official role as a caregiver began, even though I had been a caregiver for years. My ability to control my emotions during trying times would aid me while dealing with difficult situations. God has given me the ability to cast my cares like a sin into the depths of the sea. Yes, I am strong because He created me to be so. He knew that I would be able to handle these times leaning and resting in His arms. He has created this new creature so that I can walk into my destiny. Many things have to change, that is the breaking.

Some people need to leave, in order to draw you nearer to Him. Some jobs need to change – that may be your molding. I say, change me, oh Lord. Your presence and anointing is all I need. You are my savior, my way-maker, my miracle worker. That is who you are. My God, you are my everything good for me. Because all things work together for good to them that love God, to them who are called according to His purpose.

Whenever my strength is required for a situation, I pray: Lord, let me respond in a manner that is pleasing to God. Lord, take this burden, I give it to you and I trust Him to do with it how He will. At this stage in the game, I have learned to lean and trust in God because I know He will see me through and on the other side – there will be glory after this.

BIO

First and foremost, Stephanie Carter is a Woman of God. She is heir to the Kingdom of God and He is the Head of her life. She has attended Greater Word of Truth since May 2005 under the leadership of Apostle Dr. Freida Henderson. Their mission statement of GWOT has framed her life, "Winning Souls and Saving lives for Jesus Christ".

Stephanie Carter has lived in Raleigh, NC for 30 years. She has been in the nursing profession for 44 years and has earned a Bachelor of Science degree in Nursing. To enrich her education and further her understanding of her faith, she completed 2 Masters of Art degrees (Biblical Studies, and Ministerial and Pastoral Ministries).

Stephanie has always had caregiving (servitude) in her heart and spirit. As a single parent of 2 boys, she opened her home and became a foster parent in 2001. From that affiliation, she adopted a family unit (twin girls and a boy) into her home and heart.

She has endured many trials and tribulations thus far but through it all God has strengthened her so that her life can be used by Him.

Stephanie has 5 children:Darren, Nnamdi, Ta'onna, Te'onna, and Darius. She has 3 grandchildren: Elijah, Jachin, and Blair.

To God Be the Glory!

SPONSORED BREAK

CHAPTER 9

Return of the MAQ
By
Marquita Clark

For a while I couldn't remember the last time that I smiled a real smile. I was thinking, when did I feel like me? How did I, and when did I, lose Marquita? Where had she gone? It wasn't until the pandemic really hit that I had time to sit down and see me. I must admit I blamed a lot of things that were going wrong in my life in the present and in the past. I didn't take ownership of any of it because I didn't feel as though most of it was my fault. I had some things happen that I felt like I'd never recover from.

Marquita was just existing and not truly living. I didn't want that for myself anymore, I wanted more, I yearned for more, I felt like I deserved more. I was searching for something, and I didn't know what. I realized that I was searching for me – who am I? I was always a shy girl. I loved to be around people, and when I am comfortable and I truly trust people, I am the life of the party. I love to laugh and joke and be in the presence of people.

In the summer of 2003, I came out of my shell, and I was a senior in high school – geesh, that seems like years ago. I wanted to hang out with my friends more and do what I thought normal teens did. My mother was married at sixteen, so we, my siblings and I, couldn't start officially dating until we were sixteen. At that time, I thought that was just the dumbest rule ever and I couldn't believe that she was doing this to me. I already felt like the awkward one of the group.

I felt like I stood out and didn't fit in with anyone, even the few that I had. However, I went to more games, like one or two; I went to a couple of parties, not anything too radical. I was so into church and serving the Lord that my subconscious wouldn't let me do anything that was too out of my comfort zone.

That was a good thing, it kept me grounded. It kept me focused. I wanted to be a pediatric nurse. I was in my first relationship, I was on my way to college in a few months, and my parents were separated. That was one of the roughest times in my life. I felt like that was the first time that I had crawled out from under the rock, being shy and sheltered.

I went through things, but nothing like this. My example of what love is, what it looks like, was shattered. My dad was saying, "It's just a separation," but my mom, she didn't say much - she didn't have to. Her actions showed this was the end for us. Looking back, she was strong! I felt like my family was falling apart and I had to hold it together and be strong and not let anyone see my emotions because I never want anyone to pity me. That's where my mindset of if I can't do it or my parents can't do it, it won't get done came from. Some may look at it as learning to be independent and stand on your own, but it really wasn't. It was me building walls that I didn't want to ever break down.

I never wanted to feel the pain my mother felt, and I didn't want to give anyone that power to do so. This wall would be the hardest to break down. Here I am, going to college. I spent summers away with family so this should be easy, no big deal, I got this. My mom and I went to Elizabeth City to take me to my summer session, I was so scared of her leaving me there. We were eating and I was like, "Ma, I left my sheets and stuff at home, I have to go back with you." I remember one of the students saying, "Wal-Mart is around the corner, you can get some and come back, you don't want to miss the fun." In my mind, I'm thinking 'Oh no, sir, I left them on purpose, I am not staying here tonight, I'm going home.' That's exactly what we did, went home. I don't think my mom was too happy but I think she understood; she always knows how to read me.

We went back the next day and I was so excited. Well, August was fast approaching and I was NOT ready, but once again I felt like I had to be strong and I couldn't let her see my cry. I couldn't let her know how scared and nervous I was and how I wished so badly that my dad was there, but I didn't want to be ungrateful to my uncle who came and helped me move into my dorm. Man, I was a ball of emotions and did not know how to control them. I was angry, mad, sad, happy, excited, and all kinds of nervous. I think I went home every weekend because I was homesick. In my mind it was keeping me focused.

I was on the dean's list freshman year. We started a Bible study in our dorm room, we were in church every Sunday without fail. I started to get comfortable at school. I was working, I was meeting new people, I wasn't going back home as much. Well now, I'm comfortable and at home. Did I forget to mention that my boyfriend broke up with me and I started meeting new men and they were looking all delicious and handsome? And let's talk about smartness! Whew! While working at Food Lion I befriended a guy who was working there. I was truly just trying to be friendly, nothing more, nothing less. After a while I started noticing him around campus and I thought nothing of it. It wasn't until we were coming in from going out to dinner and I noticed him on my floor that I started to worry. 'He's not a student of the university, so why is he here?' was my thought.

I called my best friends and told them what was going on. After that, we started noticing him in the café, at parties, around campus – every time I turned around, he was there. I would not let him or anyone else know how scared I was. I was always saying, "I'm just a little concerned." I think my friends knew that I was more than a little concerned, they never left my side for the rest of that year. They said I should've reported him, but I didn't. Thank God that nothing serious ever came of it. This experience made me paranoid about my surroundings and I was constantly looking over my shoulder, I was extra cautious. I thought I was handling things well; I wasn't, I was just putting up walls and file cabinets. Every rejection had a wall and a cabinet that was linked to the next.

My mom got hurt on the job, and this was the excuse that I needed. My mom needed me, so I left and moved to South Carolina and didn't finish school because my mom needed me. The truth is, I needed her, I needed to be close to her. Little did I know, South Carolina was going to be the place to break me in ways that I never imagined that I'd be broken. I started dating two men and then I got serious with one, he claimed he wanted to marry me and I was so happy.

The summer of 2008 I miscarried and he was nowhere to be found. It's crazy how things work. I was trying to message him on Yahoo messenger and the picture that popped up was of him and some other woman. I was torn. My second love left me just like my dad and my first love. After that, I was looking for love from a man in all the wrong places. After a couple of years of this, I met this man. We hit it off, we were friends, and I thought we were going to be more than that, but he had another friend that he wanted to be more with. We never made anything official but to me he was my one, my person. Anyway, I started talking to this other man when I realized that he was never going to see me as more and I couldn't keep that cycle going.

So once again, I was rejected by a man that I thought loved, another folder for the file cabinet and another few bricks to add to the wall. I met another man and this one broke me. He helped us move. I will never forget November 24, 2013. I could not believe that this man that I trusted would do this to me. I could not believe that I trusted him and let this happen to me. Me? This was the hardest year of my life. I found out I had lupus and I was sexually assaulted. I was so depressed, I was so overwhelmed, I was in a dark place for a while.

I remember telling my mom that I felt like I was going to snap and I needed to get out. So much had happened from 2008 to 2015 and I needed to leave. I left South Carolina and moved back to North Carolina in 2016. I wanted to reconnect and build a better relationship with my dad and go back to school to finally earn my degree. A new beginning was just what I needed.

I moved back to North Carolina with the mindset of only being here until I finished my degree. It's 2022 and I haven't gone back to school yet. I am trusting the process. I moved back and started working and met a few men, went on some dates, and enjoyed the single life. I was still continuing the cycle; I met a man that I gave two and a half years to for him to tell me five days before Christmas to leave him alone. This time was different for me.

We'd broken up several times but this time I was over him and I didn't crawl back. I realized who I was and what I deserved and he wasn't it, so I moved on.

I met this man and we were going through some similar things so we decided to only be friends. He was NOTHING like anyone I ever dated. He was all of my nerves mixed up in one. You know the man that you say you'll never date because he has six kids, he's an addict, we fought each other a time or two, I had to call the police a time or two, etc., the man that you couldn't ever see yourself with? Yea, he was that man for me. I never had to experience this type of relationship before. I pray, but with him I prayed, I stayed before God.

This relationship humbled me, it taught me to stop passing judgment. This relationship was the last piece of the puzzle. The last relationship that I am going to allow to break me. I look at it as, it had to happen to put this puzzle together. I can't start something new without completely finishing the old because I am always going to wonder. The work that I had to do on myself helped to answer some questions to complete the puzzle.

They say you can't heal in the place where you were hurt. I believe if you allow yourself to, you can heal anywhere. The healing has to start from the inside. The pandemic was just what I needed. It gave me the time to begin that healing to get back to me. I talk to my dad more now than ever before. I started my businesses and began the hard work, the ugly work. I began knocking those walls down, cleaning out those internal file cabinets, and actually doing the work. Every day is a chance to start again, a chance to take a chance on me.

When I started taking a chance on myself, I took responsibility for the things that I've done to get me where I am, and I stopped taking responsibility for things that others have done. I opened up a little more. I smile a little more. I am getting back to Marquita. In some of the work that I do, I work with girls in helping them stay true to themselves. I tell them all the time: I will not ask you to do things that I have not done. In trusting MY process, I am piecing my purpose together. I am piecing my 'why' together. I am finding that this masterpiece called me takes time, and one piece at a time it is coming together. I am becoming and I am loving the journey back to me.

BIO

Marquita is a daughter, sister, auntie, and entrepreneur. She is the founder of MAQ Mentoring, a nonprofit organization that mentors girls. Marquita is a mentor who dedicates her time to helping young girls build their confidence and find their voice. She has seen first-hand how mentorship can change a girl's life.

Marquita is always on the go. Whether she's spending time with her family and friends, attending church events, or at home enjoying a good movie, she's always busy living life to the fullest. Writing a book has been on her bucket list for years, and eventually, with the help of her Coach, Freida Henderson, it became a reality. Marquita also loves to craft and learn something new.

WELCOME TO MAQ MENTORING

#wedothistogetHER

Marquita Clark

Owner, MAQ Mentoring

📞 **919-675-1561**

🌐 **mclark@maqmentoring.org**

CHAPTER 10

Running From Me to Start Again

By
Lavette Connelly

Therefore, since we are surrounded by such a great cloud of witnesses, let us throw off everything that hinders and the sin that so easily entangles. And let us run with perseverance the race marked out for us, fixing our eyes on Jesus, the pioneer and perfecter of faith...
Hebrew 12:1

For the past couple of weeks, I had been training for the state conference for my high school track meet with my teammates and the day had finally come. This was going to be the day I got my high school letter (C). Coach yelled, "Lavette, 400 meter run up next, get ready." I got to the start and I was ready. The start shot went off, I was winning this race, talking to myself, "Lavette you got this, just pace yourself." As I was coming around the curve on the track, I hit what they call "The Wall". Down I went, to never get up to finish the race that day.

That day, I never ran again. The next day my mom scheduled a doctor's appointment with my cardiologist – oh, did I mention I have heart disease? This was the doctor I had all through my early years and high school, he told me that day: "Aurora, You Are Just Not Going to Be Able to Do Things Like Other Kids." He went on and on talking with my mom, but I only heard "I'm different than everybody else." My mom already had dealt with me as a baby being born with birth defects, so she was very protective, sometimes overly – well, to me anyway.

I never understood that until I got older myself. It's the end of my year and the junior/school counselors were doing planning with juniors and seniors. My school counselor knew I had problems taking tests and that I had a heart condition, so she suggested that I meet with vocational rehabilitation services for after high school planning.

My mom gave permission, so I went to meet the program.

The appointment was made so I went to the vocational rehabilitation without my mom.
I was sitting in the waiting room waiting to hear my name called, "Aurora Royal." I jumped,
excited because I am feeling like I am taking care of my life planning without my mom to speak
for me. The counselor at vocational rehabilitation introduced herself to me and started to tell
me about the program and how they help people with disabilities.

When I heard the word 'disabilities', something stopped in me, "disabilities"? Was I in the right
place, and did I hear her right? All I wanted was help with my planning for my future after high
school. She opens up a folder with my records and starts to ask me about my family, parents,
and siblings. "What education do your parents have?" she asked. My dad completed his high
school diploma and my mom has her four-year college degree. I was thinking, what has that got
to do with me? This woman says to me, "Well, you want to be able to get a college degree like
your mother did.

The only place you will work well as being is a teacher assistant, but your level of
comprehension is not at a level that will get you a job of any higher level." Don't get me
wrong, there was nothing wrong with being a teacher assistant back then and there isn't
anything wrong with being one now. I just wanted something else different for me and I was
willing to work for it. Oh, did I mention that they tested me too, but I thought as a young child
that they were going to help me with those skills? Vocational rehabilitation was and is a place
that serves individuals who have a chronic disability that keeps them from getting or keeping a
job. The primary goal is to assist the person to become employed and retain their employment
for at least 90 days or more.

(Side Note) Never be afraid to get your children help, if they need it, don't look at it as your
child being labeled, keep in mind that You, the parent, have to be an advocate for your child, for
him or her to get the right services they need to be successful in life. My eyes watered up, but
I did not let a tear fall. This was my life; did I hit a brick wall again? Something came over me
and I told that lady that day: "You might not be able to help," and what kind of place is this any
way that would tell me or any other child what they cannot do or accomplish? I say I am going
to get my degree one day Ms. whatever her name was. I got up and walked out, got in my car
and cried all the way home. I was thinking, how many other kids had she said this to? I was
more determined than ever to win this race called life I was running.

As a young child back then you wanted to go to college, well at least I did. My mom, as a
single mom, exposed my brother and I to a lot of educational things, education was the key to a
successful life. She was the only one out of eight children to get her four-year degree. She
was the one everyone came to in the family to handle business and she was a country girl,
me too, but I had to go home and tell my mom I didn't want their services or their money for
nothing. My mom thought this was a way for me to pay to go to school. But at what cost?

Even at a young age I felt something wasn't right about this. If I go through this program, it will stay with me for life, I was thinking all this on my way home. I was counting up the cost back then and didn't even know it. If someone counts the cost of something that has happened or will happen, they consider how the consequences of that action or event affect them.

So it was in the natural so it is in the spirit (Luke 14: 25-33 NIV).
Large crowds were traveling with Jesus, and turning to them he said: "If anyone comes to me and does not hate father and mother, wife and children, brothers and sisters-yes, even their own life-such a person cannot be my disciple. And whoever does not carry their cross and follow me cannot be my disciple. Suppose one of you wants to build a tower.

Won't you first sit down and estimate the cost to see if you have enough money to complete it? For if you lay the foundation and are not able to finish it, everyone who sees it will ridicule you, saying, "this person began to build and wasn't able to finish." Or suppose a king is about to go to war against another king. Won't he first sit down and consider whether he is able with ten thousand men to oppose the one coming against him with twenty thousand? If he is not able, he will send a delegation while the others are still a long way off and will ask for terms of peace. In the same way, those of you who do not give up everything you have cannot be my disciples."

I know in this scripture Jesus was saying, if you want to be a disciple, you're going to have to let some things go that might mean a lot to you. And follow me for WHO I AM and not what you can get. Jesus knew back then, as He knows today, that He has to have disciples with some staying power when things get a little tough. Well I told my mom what that lady had said to me and that I was not ever going back to that place again. If I do it's only to show her my degree. My mom didn't say anything; she knew I was hurt.

As I was getting ready to start running, that year I graduated with honors and received two scholarships for college. I had met this guy over the summer and he was my first love. I was young and in love and he was older. I was working on my associate's degree full-time and working part-time at a childcare center. I was living the good life, I had an older guy, and little did I know that this older man was married and everyone was telling my mom, and I didn't believe them.

That was a whole mess within itself. Every time I asked him if he was married he said no, and I believed him. But people were telling my mom I told him, he said they just wanted for him to talk to them. After a year and a half of dating I finally said, "Look, are you married or not because if you are I don't want to be with you anymore, and now people are saying you got a baby on the way." I was like, "Look, I am young and I don't have to be with you anymore. If you don't get a divorce we can't be together." Well in less than six months he got that divorce.

This was somewhere I always wanted to go, I was getting ready to go off to Bennett College in Greensboro. I went and loved it. Every single day I got a phone call all times of day and night from my man. I was like, girl he really loves me. I had come home one weekend and we were driving downtown in Raleigh, and he threw a little box at me and said, "Open." I just said, "Yes." I got a ring. I left Bennett College to come back home to be with him, I enrolled back in community college and planned my wedding for a year. Right after we got married he started to smoke, I had never seen him pick up a cigarette in five and a half years!!!! He said I didn't smoke around you because I knew you didn't like it. What else was I in for, I thought.

One day I was in the kitchen cooking and calling my grandma about how to cook something. I was excited and loved to cook, I had all the food in the pans on the stove, he was watching TV, wow I remember it like it was yesterday. He called me, "Lavette, come here," and said, "My mom cooked and we have to go there and eat." I said, "But I have all the food in the pans." He said "They might make me choose." I walked away and went back to the kitchen, I just couldn't understand. I went back to the room where he was and stood at the doorway and said, "I left my family to start a family with you, and if it's that hard for you to feel like you got to choose, don't choose me," and walked away, he didn't even come after me.

That was the day I started slowly backing away from ME. In Joshua 24:15 NIV: "But if serving the Lord seems undesirable to you, then choose for yourselves this day whom you will serve, whether the gods your ancestors served beyond the Euphrates, or the gods of the Amorites, in whose land you are living. But as for me and my household, we will serve the Lord." I am not saying that he had to serve me or anything like that, but it was the principle of the matter. We had been through a lot for the past couple of years. I finished with my associates degree and was working as a director of a childcare center. As a matter of fact, this was the same center I was working at in high school. I worked my way up and became their director. I always felt that the man should have the plan, being the head of the household and all.

When I saw that was not working I tried for us or me to do a plan so we could work to grow our marriage; you build on some things. I just began to take the lead in the marriage, working two jobs, asking family for money to help me pay what I could not cover. I had just got paid and left my purse in the car, he said, "Ill be right back." I said, "Bring me my purse, I got it." He had it alright, my purse came back with no money, and he didn't know what happened. I still believed him. After looking back, how could I have been so naive? He started having these nose bleeds and they happened a lot.

We had the same doctor so I suggested that he make an appointment to check his blood pressure. He went to the doctor so many times that I didn't even know about that. One day he told me that our doctor told him she was not going to see him anymore if he didn't get his health together. I was upset with her, saying, "She can't tell you that, she is supposed to help you regulate your blood pressure." I was going to report her.

He said no she was just doing her job. One day I had to go to the doctor and she said to me, "I think you should take an AIDS test." I said, "Why, I'm married and my husband was the only person I had been with." I did take the test and it was negative and she said to me, "Take it again in five years and then another five years."

I left the doctor's office that day confused. That was over fifteen years ago. I was blinded by what I wanted to see and believe; this man had a cocaine habit that I didn't even see. As women we tend to see what we want to, even at the cost of our very own life. One day he had written me this poem called "Lifesaver". I remember him reading it to me, the end was something like: "When I sit back off the shores and look to see, the "Lifesaver" for me was really my wife." Sometimes as women we must realize we can't run the race of life forgetting about ourselves.

I started back going to school to complete my four-year degree and started going to church even if I went alone. I made sure the house was clean and food was done before I left the house, even when he was coming on Sunday more while I was going to church, I never argued, I prayed. God saved my ex-husband and we got full custody of His child. I stopped school for the second time when my ex-husband needed to go back to school for his four-year degree.

I felt someone had to be home, it was me. I felt alone a lot of times and wanted an out after 15 years of marriage and he was an ordained Reverend at the time. I left, moved to another county, and did my so-called thing at the time. I was running from my very own self and didn't know how to start again. After that I felt as if I had spent enough time looking at the past, cherishing memories, and learning lessons. I was trying my own self to heal wounds of past hurts that caused pain in another man's arms. Wrong thing to do, ladies.

The devil will use you against you to hurt your own self by putting thoughts in your own mind that you are not good enough to run or finish your own race; it was like I was hitting that brick wall again. I remember wanting, needing, to find a church in the county that I moved to. Little did I know that a church right down the road from me saved my life and changed my life forever. When I heard this lady pastor say "Say when you come to this church you have lost the right to fall", her message that day was "HELP I'm Stuck." That day was the day I wanted to start Running AGAIN.

BIO

Author Aurora Lavette Connell is a native of Clayton, North Carolina. She has been a member of "Greater Word of Truth" for fifteen years. Where she was the director of ministry of the faith-based child development center. Lavette has always loved children and has a heart for children and their needs. She is currently working as an Mental Health Disability Specialist for Head Start. Lavette is a strong leader in her family and she loves them and her church family.

She loves traveling, cooking, and trying different types of foods. Lavette wants to remind other women as she had to remind herself, of the woman you/she can be and will be, just somewhere along the way the woman in you/me/she got lost.

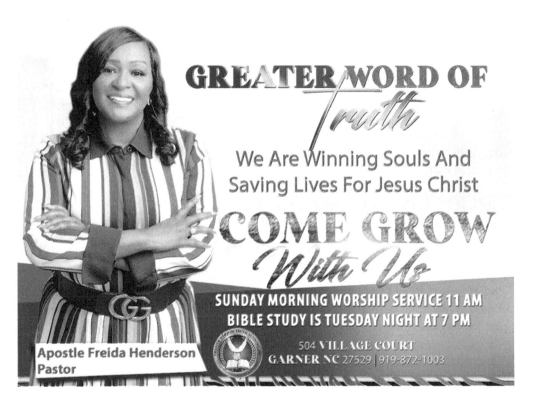

CHAPTER 11

Don't Quit Before The Miracle Happens

By
LeCole Keaton

For over 20 years I suffered from depression. There were also times when I wanted to take my life. I was in denial about it. Doctors tried to put me on medication, but it didn't work. I took myself off the medication and decided I would try to deal with it myself. During this time, I would look at others and how happy they were and how God was blessing them. Listening to them tell their testimonies on the goodness of Jesus. I asked God, "When is my turn? Why am I still suffering? Why am I fighting an ongoing battle in my MIND? Why, Lord, why?" Oh, I would have pity parties when I was alone, thinking I didn't matter and that no one loved me. Wondering why I was alone and hurt.

Trying to find comfort, love, and security in a man and hoping that they could help bring me out of my state of depression. Have you heard of the song that goes, 'Looking for love in all the wrong places and in too many faces?' Yes, that was me. At one point I was dealing with so many men that I would brag about how many men I had at any given time. I used to compare myself to a basketball team. I have a starting five and a bench! Yes, I was proud of it, and at that particular time in my life you could not tell me anything. But the depression was still there.

I ended up blaming men for the state I was in and deflecting from the real issue. The enemy tried, and he tried to get me to give up on God. To stay in the comfortable yet miserable state I was in. For years I had an ongoing battle within my mind. I needed deliverance, but how do I get deliverance, Lord? I was reminded of words to a song that my mother and grandmother used to sing: "We come this far by faith, leaning on the Lord, trusting in His Holy word, He's never failed me yet! OH, can't turn around!"

Wow, I said to myself, God has brought me too far to give up! God spoke to me and said, "I have need of you." I said, "Me? No Lord, I am a mess, I am insecure, and I have done and gone through so much in my life! I am not ready, Lord! Why me?" God said, "Why not you?" I said, "God, I can't see it!" God said to me, "Don't quit before the miracle happens."

God reminded me when I was married to my first husband. My first husband was physically abusive. At that time, I had my daughter and my oldest son, and I was pregnant with my third child. There were times I didn't know if I was going to live or if my children were going to live. I was so scared all I could do was pray for God's protection over me and my children. I slept with a knife in between my mattress. My mother begged me to leave him. But I told her no, the Bible speaks against divorcing. My mother told me, yes it does, but not if your spouse is abusing you.

My mother also told me about a dream she had that she had to go to the morgue to identify my body. I got so angry with her. I said to her that he was not going to kill me because he loved me. I was wrong, so very wrong. One morning I was getting my children ready for school; I was six months pregnant at the time. We got into an argument. I sent my children to my mother-in-law's house who lived across the street from us. After the children left, we continued to argue. The next thing I knew he had grabbed me by my throat, lifted me off the ground, and threw me down on the bed. I turned on my side so that he would not injure the baby.

I couldn't breathe, I couldn't speak, or yell. All I could do was think Jesus, save me! Jesus, save me and my baby! When I did, he jumped up off me. My mother's dream began to resonate with me. I had to get out and I had to get out as soon as possible. The next day I began to feel pain in my neck, my elbow, and my ribs. I was injured and I did not realize it. I told him I was hurt and I needed to go to the emergency room. He begged me not to go to the emergency room and apologized for hurting me. He watched my every move that evening. But I had already set a plan into place. I knew I was taking a risk, but I also knew God was with me. I had my parents pick my children up from school and take them to their house. I knew that he was going to do his usual routine of drinking until he got drunk and then passing out. When he did, I packed a bag with clothes for me and my children. Got in the car, left, and went to the emergency room.

I was numb but relieved at the same time. When I got to the emergency room, I let them know what had happened and they immediately contacted the police. After the doctor examined me, he told me I had a sprained elbow for which I needed to wear a sling. I had strained muscles in the back of my neck and bruised ribs. My baby was not harmed and had a strong and healthy heartbeat. The situation could have been much worse, but God had a plan for me. God delivered me out of that situation.

I said to God, "Yes, you delivered me from that situation and I thank you." God said, "You didn't quit, going through that entire situation you still believed. Even when you were being choked, you couldn't breathe or speak, but all you had to do was think, Jesus! Save me and my baby! I saved you and your child!" I was speechless. I could not say a word.

I had called on the Lord and He heard my cry, even though my cry was not verbal, He still heard it! I began to cry. I then thought of the story of Elijah and the widow woman (1 Kings 17:8-16 AMP). God sent Elijah to the city of Zarephath and once he got there he found a widow woman. When Elijah arrived, he saw the widow woman gathering sticks for firewood. Elijah called out to her and asked her to bring him some water and some bread. The woman told him that she had no bread, only a handful of flour and a little oil in the jar, and she was going to bake it for her and her son's last meal and then die. Elijah told her not to be afraid and instructed her to continue with her plans and to make him a little bread first and bring it out to him and then make herself one and then her son one.

For the Lord God of Israel said that the bowl of flour will not run low, nor shall the jar of oil be empty until the Lord sends rain again. The widow did as Elijah instructed her. She and her family were able to eat for many days, the flour did not run low, nor did the oil in the jar become empty according to the word the Lord spoke through Elijah. I began to understand and see what God was trying to show me. The widow woman was ready to give up and die, but God had another plan. God had need of her to make sure she took care of the man of God.

God has need of me so that I can be a blessing to others. Now, I understand. I cannot give up now. Just because the miracle has not happened, doesn't mean that it won't! He was preparing me. I had to come out of that slump I was in and I did! Thank God for both my natural mother and my Apostle, who is also my spiritual mother and currently my life coach, for never quitting or giving up on me and keeping me in prayer. On a Sunday service back in 2019, my Apostle had me come up to the stand in front of the congregation. Then she told me to walk back and forth and had the church to applaud for me. She said, "You all take a good look at her now, because in a year, she will not look the same!" I was thinking to myself, Lord, look different how? My outer appearance or my inner appearance? He said to me, "Trust the process."

Now, here is the kicker to this. I was thinking that I was going to get through the process without doing any work during the process. I also thought this was going to be an overnight success story and that I was not going to endure any pain during the process. I was wrong. I had to get over myself to help myself.
In the past I would blame others for my shortcomings, how I felt, and for my behavior. Worried about what other people were doing and not doing. How in the world was I going to help others when I could not even help myself? Yes, that same insecure thought! I was sick and tired of overthinking and overreacting. I was still hurting from things that happened in the past. I had not fully healed and was walking about with a band-aid.

What I needed to do was to change my mindset and to heal. However, the first thing that I needed to do was acknowledge that I had a problem. Next, I needed to ask God to forgive me and to forgive myself. These steps were key and vital to changing my mindset and to the healing process. I started to receive life coaching, and those old wounds opened back up. It began to expose some things that I didn't want to deal with, but it had to be done. Issues with insecurity, self-identity, low self-esteem, and confidence, just to name a few. I had to press on and endure. If God brings you to it,

He will surely bring you through it! So I pressed onward! Trusting God and the process. One of the things that I wanted to stop was taking anxiety medicine. I was taking it once, sometimes twice a day. Let me tell you, there were days that I wanted to give up and quit! I had sleepless nights plagued with anxiety, crying, and overthinking. But with the help of God and my life coach, I am no longer on anxiety medication. I learned how to overcome anxiety. Anxiety is fear and I know that God has not given me the spirit of fear, but of power and of love and of a sound mind (2 Timothy 1:7).

A sound mind, a mind that is at peace. Yes, that is what I need! So, if I feel anxiety trying to arise, I tell myself, NO! I am not going to do this today! I am not going to allow fear to disrupt my life or my peace! God has need of me! Yes! A constant reminder! An affirmation that God needs me to help others just like me! That aha moment! I have a purpose. I was blessed to be a blessing!

When I realized that I had a purpose and what my purpose was, I asked God, "What are my next steps?" God said, "Continue to work on yourself and as you work on yourself the rest will follow." I wasn't sure exactly what was to come, but I was trusting God and trusting the process. I began meeting with an image consultant and continued with my life coaching. My confidence grew, I was changing inside and out, and I started to come out of my comfort zone.

In February 2022, my life coach encouraged me to do something that I had never done before. I thought of doing something easy like cooking a meal that I had never cooked before, but no, I needed something more challenging. A few days after the challenge was presented, my daughter was telling me of an opportunity to do some plus-size modeling. I said, "THAT'S IT!" This is definitely something that I had never done before. Modeling? I was nervous, because even though it was plus-size modeling, I was older and not sure if I would make the cut.

However, I still gave it a shot! I sent in 3 pictures and waited to hear if I had made it to the second round. Not only did I make it through the first round, I made it through the second round and was picked as a model for a virtual fashion show. I was also asked to be a brand ambassador for the plus-size boutique I was modeling for. The opportunities snowballed! I was asked to do other fashion shows and photoshoots! I definitely was not expecting any of this to happen. God gets all the glory!

As I continue to grow, I pray each and every day that I may minister and be a blessing to someone. That they may see Christ in me. I began posting encouraging and inspirational messages on social media and sending them out at least once a week on my job. When I started doing this I began to receive messages from people about how my posts encouraged them and blessed them. One particular message I received was from a coworker, who told me that there would be days when they did not know how they would make it through, and then I would send out an encouraging post and it would help them make it through the day! At that moment, I thought that everything that I had gone through was for this moment!

For me to tell someone who was down and didn't think they were going to make it that everything was going to be alright! All I could do was thank and praise God. Every conversation that I had with God came back to me! Lord, I now understand. I understand why I went through and experienced the things I did. I understand why I needed to be patient and trust the process.

Thankful that my experience with my first ex-husband did not go another way. Thankful for the times I wanted to give up but I didn't! Lord, I am so glad that I didn't quit before the miracle happened! To everyone that is reading this: no matter what you may be going through, be encouraged. God has not forgotten! God is in the neighborhood and your miracle is on the way! So don't quit before the miracle happens! Thank you, Jesus!

BIO

LeCole Keaton was born and raised in Raleigh NC. LeCole has 4 children. Kelsey Armstrong, Cameron Shaw, Corey Merritt, and Caelan Hodge. She is a graduate of The University of Phoenix with an Associates degree in psychology, a graduate of Safe Haven Bible College with an Bachelor's Degree in Biblical Studies, and currently pursuing her Masters degree for a degree in Biblical Studies.

LeCole has worked full time as a Medical Information Associate I for 4 years and recently received the Energizer Award from the company, for encouraging, uplifting and keeping her teammates motivated. While working full time, LeCole has taken her hobby of making decorative wreaths and made it into a business.

LeCole is a survivor of domestic violence and loves to help and encourage others who are currently going through or coming out of a similar situation. LeCole is a nurturer, has a heart for women and wants to help them grow.

SPONSORED BREAK

CHAPTER 12
From Promiscuous To Pray
By
Sonya Hall

"If anyone ever touches you inappropriately, let me know," is what I was always told as a child until I gave birth at age 16. Molested at a young age but not understanding, nor did I know what the word meant. Raised by my grandfather, AKA "Daddy", and his wife, AKA "Mommy", and my Aunt Diane who took care of us, who is still alive today, I was protected, shielded, loved and prayed over from birth to age 7 – and I thank you from the bottom of my heart.

At age 7, who knew that moving to White Plains NY would change my entire life. I was too young to understand why I was leaving "Mommy and Daddy" and the area I knew so well as Spanish Harlem. In this new place I would have to make new friends and adjust to people. I had a certain uneasy feeling at such a young age, after all I was too young to understand what was going on. Unfortunately, parts of my life were blocked out from me, and it is probably for the best. But what I do remember at age 14 I caught myself liking this guy who I just knew was handsome. I thought he was the best thing since pizza and ice cream.

I remember being so naïve when he took me into one of our friend's rooms, who knew it would be my first time having intercourse? I remember it so well because it was on Easter Sunday and I had on the cutest dress. I remember us being in the room and he lifted my dress, and I just laid there thinking, what is he doing? Not fully understanding the pain I was feeling, or enduring, was because I was a virgin. The sad thing is you always hear about it in Health where they would discuss sex education, but they never gave the full details of how it would happen.

After all, I had not come into my womanhood until later in my 14 years of age. The problem was I always hung out with the older crowd because I was mature for my age; him being 2 years older was no surprise. Let me just say this, it all happens so quick, but would be the start of my promiscuity.

He was my first, my first love, my first hurt, my first everything. So having the urge to be loved and getting rid of that urge, promiscuity became my name at the tender age of 15; we would have sex on top of the roof, in the basement, in the garage at the mall, at the school, in friends' apartments, any and everywhere.

Promiscuous became my name. Suddenly, it all stopped, and he was no longer interested in me but was pursuing someone else. Then the storm came, stomach hurting, vomiting, and getting bigger by the day. Uncertain of what the situation was because I was still getting my menstrual cycle. At the time, my grandmother AKA Ma Fats, took me to her own doctor who advised that I was pregnant. Pregnant at age 15 and certain who the father was because of the time. Boy, was I wrong. When my ex and I broke it off I immediately started sleeping with someone else.

If you are reading this, then you know that promiscuity will have you not knowing who the father is if you are having multiple partners. Let me explain: the Oxford dictionary states that promiscuous means "having or characterized by many transient sexual relationships". After having my son, I became more promiscuous just because I could. Now that I had a baby, the door was open. Even If I didn't want to have sex I would, but what I learned to do was not be in a relationship because that meant that I would be tied down to someone that I did not want to give my heart to.

I wanted to do what men were doing back then, stick, and move. Whomever I pursued or if they pursued me, if I wanted them, I could have them. Then one day at age 18, after already sleeping with over 10-15 men, I was raped. Never thought this person would do that to me as I told them NO. I never flirted with this person nor anything else because he was dating a friend of mine. Back then I couldn't tell, and who would believe me?

After all I did have a child and was known as a fast tail girl. I said nothing and became pregnant with his baby. He made sure that I did not keep it, he even took me to the abortion clinic himself. After all, I didn't want the baby, I could hardly take care of the one I had. Remember Promiscuity can cause you to have multiple abortions or miscarriages. This is when I questioned GOD. Why me, why did I have to go through all this? Why did I have to go through being accused of sleeping with someone else's man or husband?

Why was I the one being called names from women who didn't even know me, who wanted to fight me over a man that I didn't even want? Why did I always have to fight for my life? I questioned GOD because of the things that had gone on and had been going on in my life. I knew who GOD was because I stayed in church regardless of where I was. But I wanted to know why GOD made me the way I was, why He seemed to set me up for failure. I felt like I had been cheated out of life. After all, I wasn't the prettiest thing on the block, I had a chipped tooth and short hair and didn't look like much. I just couldn't understand why.

At age 21, I finally got into a serious relationship, so I thought. However, this person wasn't giving me the attention that I needed. He was staying out late, being seen with another woman at a club. So, one day I had enough and told him it was over. He threw my clothing out the window, but he never put his hands on me. My best friend, who is a male, came over to make sure I was ok. The next incident would not end up so great with a different relationship because he became obsessed.

During a bad winter storm my then-boyfriend and I got into an argument about me going to the pay phone to let my job know I was not coming in because I had no one to watch my son. I asked him to watch my son while I went to the payphone to call the job since my phone was off. He said, "I am not watching that 'bastard'." He was upset because I refused to have a baby with him. I told him to get out, because I was not about to let him talk about my child like that. He got up in my face and poked me, I lost my mind, I punched him in the mouth, we began to fight. I ended up pulling him on top of me, I was punching for my life.

My son came into the room and jumped on his back and yelled, "Get off my mommy." As he raised up his arm to hit my child, strength came from GOD and I was able to push my son out of the way. I told him to go downstairs to my neighbor's house and call the cops. My son didn't want to leave me, but I made him go. Next thing I did was grab the aluminum baseball bat and told him, "One of us is going to die today and it won't be me, but if it should happen my son will be well taken care of." I began swinging the bat and, as he ran out the back door and jumped off the balcony, I was reaching for my gun.

Yes, at age 14 my grandmother, AKA Ma Fats, AKA Hatchet woman, gave me a black and green with silver 22 handgun. My grandmother always told me, "Never let a man put his hands on you because he could kill you and you could bleed on the inside of your body." So, I kept that belief. Here I go again, GOD, why me? Why do I always have to fight for my life? So, during this time I used my neighbor's phone and called my mother to let her know what had happened and that I was bringing my son down there. At this time all my male family were in jail and I was not scared.

So, I went down to my grandmother's house and while down there he called to say sorry, and he wanted to talk. But he lost his mind when he got threatened when someone said that if they ever saw him, they would kill him. An hour later, I received a call from my neighbor letting me know that my apartment was on fire. Now let me just say, I did not belong to a church at this time, but I was singing in a choir and trying to get my life together.

The next day I went to the apartment to see what I could salvage, he had burnt everything in my bedroom and my son's room, everything had been damaged in the entire house, the only thing that did not even have a smell of smoke was my choir robes that had been hanging in the closet by the front door. When I tell you, I know that it was GOD showing me that He had a plan for my life, I knew that right then I had to do a full turnaround.

How many of you know that promiscuity can have a person love you so much they become obsessed and tell you that no one else can have you, that they will kill you themselves before they let anyone have you? GOD, thank you for my Aunt Shirly Hall who had been inviting me to church, and at that time I finally said that I would go. I went to church with what I had, a short skirt and top. I felt underdressed as the people were looking at me, but my aunt assured me, she said, "Come as you are." I'll never forget the day I went to the church, Mt Zion Holiness Church, God of America's.

This man of GOD, the 1st pastor I ever served under called me out. He spoke over my life and told me that GOD was calling me and that I had a call on my life. Did I want to hear that? Absolutely NOT. That day I gave my life over to GOD. After several years in the ministry my life had changed, I ended up doing my initial sermon but cannot remember when it was because, again, some things I cannot remember. The sad thing is I can remember what I wore only because I had the suit years later hanging in my closet. But in 2002 the tragic loss of my grandmother took a toll on me; I was there when she took her last breath, and she gave her life to CHRIST. This changed my entire life.

I was ready to do ministry, so I thought, and there came another setback. After years of learning to pray, cast out demons, usher in the spirit of the Lord through psalm, speaking in tongues, sold out, prayer cap wearing, dress down to the ankles, being delivered from promiscuity, here came the big boom. My pastor calls me out and tells me that I have a demon that I was born with that was passed down from generations and that it had to come out today. Oh my GOD, could this be the answer I was looking for? NO.

This was something else, this was a generational curse that was placed on my family that had to be broken by me. Here I go again, WHY me, GOD, why now, GOD? After all that I had done in ministry, GOD, you allowed me to be Superintendent of Sunday school, sing on the praise team, be over the Young People Institute, over the young girl's dance ministry, in charge of the jr. ushers, the young people's Sunday school teacher – after all of this, WHY now, GOD?

As I began to run through the church while my pastor was talking, all I yelled was, "Whatever this thing is, get it out of me. Remove it, GOD." Next thing I know, the demon was cast out; I was laying on the floor. Meeting was called a week later; I asked the question, "If you knew this demon was there, why did you allow me to operate in ministry?" I was told GOD had to tell him when it was time to cast out the demon. At this point, people were advised to stay away from me.

Not understanding the rejection, not being given answers may have you go back out into the world and back to whatever you were doing before, such as promiscuity. All I can tell is you GOD never gave up on me.

It was prayer that saved my life in 2008 when I met a woman then named Pastor Freida Cates who spoke into and over my life and has continued to speak over my life. It was the prayer and the laying of hands on me from a righteous woman, Apostle Freida Henderson, that said, "You are the Apple of GOD'S eye."

Did my life change instantly? NO. I can tell you this, the prayers out of her mouth from GOD's heart to my ears is what kept me. I wanted to give up, quit, run away, but didn't. I had to stay in the process and pass the test. I had to fast and pray for GOD to keep my mind, body, and soul stayed on Him. I had to learn how to fall on my knees and tell GOD I was weak, and I needed Him, I had to learn how to tell myself that I was more than enough.

I had to cry out to GOD and spare not. I had to read His word, absorb His word, feel His word, believe the prayers, and hear the voice of GOD. My prayer is that whoever reads this chapter knows that GOD can do a turnaround because He loves you. Whenever the enemy tries to attack me, I know how to pray; prayer is essential, it is the key to your turnaround, while you are praying, GOD is hearing you. Go through the process, He knows your heart. Psalms 17:8 KJV: "Keep me as the apple of the eye, hide me under the shadow of thy wings." May GOD Bless you and keep you!

BIO

Allow me to introduce myself, my name is Sonya Desneke Hall. Raised in Harlem, NY, and grew up in Winbrook Projects in White Plains, NY. I give honor to my Parents for birthing me.
I am a Mother of one son, Dawon D Hall who is married to my beautiful Daughter in Love Tekah Hall "AKA Tekah boo. Grandmother of 3. Love all my 6 siblings. I beat the statistics of being a teenage mother by finishing high school and then going on to college where I major in Business Administration and Minor in Psychology.

In my early years I've had the pleasure of singing with some famous gospel artist and being in some wonderful gospel choirs. I had the honor of being a braid Artist, cosmetologist to some famous people that you may know. I currently have a Bachelor of Arts Degree in Biblical Studies, will have a Master's Degree of Art in Biblical Studies in June 2023.

I am a Notary Public and work in Loan Servicing. While on this journey, I am praying that the work I have done naturally and spiritually has impacted someone's life in a great way. I want everyone to know that they are the Apple of God's Eye.

SPONSORED BREAK

919 400.2807
homeplatoonceo@gmail.com
cheftip@icloud.com

Services
Home Platoon offers many services for inside and outside the house. Some of those services include painting, landscaping, replacing siding, staining wood, and many more. Full list inside.

CHAPTER 13

You're Looking at An Overcomer

By

Janet Scott

Talk about an overcomer – I was born one. I was born on May 5, 1953. I came into this world an overcomer. At birth, my heart kept beating when the Lord called my twin sister to heaven. I always wondered why I made it and my twin sister did not. What made me so special? Wondering how different my life would have been if she was still alive. I often reminisce about the time and memories we would have made together.

Despite feeling cheated, God still blessed me with 6 siblings to walk through life with. I continued to overcome so many obstacles in my life. From walking a few miles to school when I was younger to one of the biggest heartbreaks of my life. I will forever be an overcomer. That's what this thing called life is all about. We are here to overcome and conquer. Each and every trial we go through is tailor made for each of us. Trials and tribulations shape and mold our characters into what God wants us to be. I've learned as long as I draw close to God, I can get through any and everything!

I survived the riots in the 60s from the assassinations of JFK and MLK. The devastation it caused to my community was catastrophic. I was living in a world of segregation where I was ostracized because of the color of my skin. I had to overcome oppression and a sense of fear just to be able to walk outside of my house. I have overcome diversity in this world, so that my children would not have to experience what I had to endure through my youth. I marched for the freedoms that we enjoy today.

As a teenager I was arrested for marching for civil rights, something I strongly believed in. At the tender age of fourteen I made a conscious decision to move to Greenville, NC.

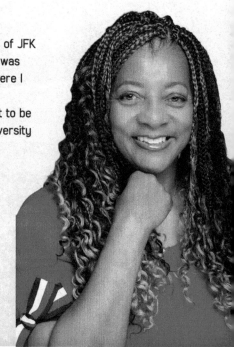

I used to spend the summers with my grandmother, which made me decide to move from the hustle of the city in Baltimore, MD. Living with my grandmother helped shape and mold my character. Working in the tobacco fields during the hot summer months was gurling.
I had work just to clothe myself for school.

Working taught me the true definition of perseverance and gave me a solid foundation of a work ethic. I finished up my schooling living with my beloved grandmother, Mama Queen. I loved her dearly. My mother was told in my youth that birthing children would be impossible for me. So, I always grew up believing that I would never have the privilege of becoming a mother. It hurt me to my core. I went through a lot of self-destruction. I was devastated, thinking that I would never have a family.

This led me through a phase of self-sabotaging behaviors. I was raised in the church, but at this point in my life I strayed away from the path God laid before me. This was not actually the first time I allowed what I was going through to dictate my relationship with God. I used the church as a revolving door. When I was going through anything in my life I would run to church. When things were going great, I left God and did my own thing.

I met the love of my life – at least I thought he was – at the age of 28. I met him at a social gathering. I was introduced to him by my best friend Sherry. Sherry and Lamar were old classmates. It was a whirlwind romance. He instantly swept me off my feet. Lamar and I lived an hour and thirty minutes away from each other. Lamar lived in Durham, NC while I lived in Greenville, NC.

Back then I lived for the weekend. All week my stomach was in knots waiting to see my man. I would catch the greyhound bus every weekend, filled with excitement. Our feelings for each other grew each week with every kiss and every hug that we shared. Once we became intimate, it was a wrap for my sanity. Nobody couldn't tell me anything about Lamar. When we were together, we were in our own world. He was my own personal drug, and I wasn't going to detox EVER!

Seven months into our relationship we couldn't stand the thought of being away from each other. I packed my bags and headed to Durham, NC to start my new life with my love. Shortly after we moved in together, he took me to New Jersey to meet his family. I vaguely remember having a conversation with his sister where she alluded to the fact that he fathered two children before he moved to Durham (first red flag ignored). Now at this point Lamar had me so wrapped up he could have told me the sky was purple and I would have believed him.

While on the drive back, I asked him about this he firmly denied it, telling me he and his sister didn't get along and she just didn't want to see him happy.

Looking back at this situation I can clearly see this was the beginning of his manipulation. Hindsight is 20/20. Naturally when you date someone you are introduced to friends and acquaintances of your significant other. Being new to the area, I really wanted to make Durham feel like home and I began to develop new friendships. I was introduced by Lamar to one of his female co-workers who was also a part-time hairstylist.

I noticed that Karen and Lamar were extremely close, but I thought nothing of it because she was also married and had a family of her own (second red flag ignored). We eventually became good friends, and she started doing my hair. We went on couple trips together and frequently had couple date nights with each other.

Eventually Lamar proposed and I said yes. We also found out we were pregnant a few weeks later.

I was over the moon and knew God had healed my womb. We had a beautiful baby girl named Samantha. I was the happiest I had been in a long time. We tied the knot shortly after Samantha was born. Two years later, I gave birth to another beautiful baby girl. We named her Ashley. As the children got older, I felt something in my life was missing. I started going back to church, bringing my children with me. Years later, Lamar decided to join church with us. He joined the male choir and life was great, or so I thought.

Throughout the years Lamar and I continued sharing our lives together, raising our girls. Our friendship with Karen and her family remained tight knit. Which is why I was beside myself when I caught them kissing in the parking lot of the gas station down the street from our house. It was one of the most embarrassing moments of my life. Myself and a few ladies from church, along with my oldest daughter Samantha, decided to have a ladies day. We went to get our nails done and went out to eat for lunch. Before being dropped off at home, Monica decided to get some gas. As we drove up to the gas station, I noticed Lamar's truck.

My friend Monica looked at me and said, "Is that Lamar?" I got out of the vehicle and walked to his truck only to see Karen and Lamar kissing. For him it was like a relief that everything was out in the open. He immediately moved into an apartment with his mistress, leaving me and my youngest daughter at our family home. By this time, my oldest had moved out and was starting a family of her own. I tried everything to keep my marriage of 22 years together. I put my pride to the side and begged Lamar to come home.

My pleas fell on deaf ears. As time went on, I became a shell of the woman I was before. I slowly started to lose my mind. I fell into a deep depression. I felt so empty. I ended up leaving the church I was a member of for so many years. I was lost and couldn't find my way back.

I started dating a year after our divorce was final. I wanted to feel anything but this emptiness day in and day out.

I met a guy named Mike through his sister who was a co-worker of mine. We were out in these streets acting a fool. Smoking and drinking, partying like there was no tomorrow. We shacked up for two years. We were introduced to a church that changed our lives forever. We started attending services regularly.

Slowly but surely, God started to mend my broken soul. Proving to me what I knew all along, that He never left me. Looking back at all the things I had to go through to get to this point in my life, God has been so faithful. I can see how the Lord has been guiding. Great is His faithfulness. I just want to encourage others that no matter what obstacles you face in life, if you hold onto God's unchanging hand, He will see you through. Draw close to Him, and when you make it to the other side you will be transformed into a creature with unwavering faith.

BIO

Janet Scott is a faithful woman of God. She is married to Deacon Frederick Scott and has three beautiful daughters. Keshia, Ashley and Nerrissa. She is the grandmother to nine grandchildren. Jason, Anthony, Aniya, Kelvin, Adrian, Amir, Victoria, Autumn, and Kyrie. She has been a member of Greater Word of Truth for 16 years. At Greater Word of Truth her Pastor Dr. Apostle Freida Henderson tells everyone when they walk through the door you have lost the right to fail! That saying has kept her throughout the years.

She truly loves God. She evangelizes everywhere she goes weather in the hair salon, the nail shop, the grocery store, or on her job she will talk to you about Jesus! Her mission is to spread the gospel of almighty living God. Her passion is to teach, shape, and help mold children. She started off as a summer camp counselor working with children. She was a counselor for over ten years. Her passion for children eventually took her into the school system. She worked in the school system with special needs children for over twenty-five years.

After retirement, her passion to help shape and mold the lives of our future generation just didn't stop when she retired. She went back to teaching children at Faith Assembly Christian Academy for a number of years. She is a true definition of an intercessor. She not only stands in the gap for others through prayer but with her time, finances, food whatever a person need if she can help she will.

You can always count on her. She always pays it forward. When she is not at church or work, she enjoys spending time with her grandchildren continuing to help shape and mold the minds of the future generation.

CHAPTER 14

It Had To Happen
By
Dr. Freida Henderson

Hello, my name is Freida Henderson and It Had to Happen! Somethings have to happen and we will not always understand why. Have you ever wondered why bad things happen to good people? Have you ever been in a state of why me?

Life can take a turn and you find yourself dealing with "how did I get here; I didn't ask for this." I looked at Esther and she found herself in a place she didn't want to be, but she had purpose. God used her to save her people; she decided to trust God and step out on faith. Esther 4:16, "If I perish, I perish", she rejected the spirit of fear. Like Esther we should never allow the spirit of fear to win. Esther was a woman of great power, but she didn't know it in the beginning.

God gave her favor with the King, but she had favor with the King of Kings, our Lord and Savior long before she knew what was going to happen in her life. Like Esther the Lord will take your tragedy and turn it into triumph. I found out the enemy doesn't care if you have boldness and confidence; he just doesn't want you to fulfill your God- given mandate.

Now, let's talk a little bit more about me. There was a time in my life when I was known as the divorced minister. However, I was faithful in the ministry, and I was an entrepreneur. Yet, at times I was finding it hard to keep a roof over my kid's head; but God always made a way.

Several years later, I would be called to pastor, but I fought that tooth and nail. One night as I laid on the floor crying and asking God what was wrong, why hadn't I been able to sleep for the last thirty days, and telling him nothing was right in my life; I received a response. I heard the Holy Spirit say, "And nothing is going to be right until you do what you have been called to do."

My reply was, "but I don't have a husband and I don't have any money; how am I going to do it?" Then the spirit of the Lord replied to me, "Not by might, nor by power, but it's by my spirit, saith the Lord". Zechariah 4:6.

I must be honest; I didn't know this was a scripture when the Holy Spirit spoke it to me. I was like, "Okay, I don't know what that really means, but yes Lord. The next day I spoke with my Bishop and he confirmed the message. He said, yes, the Lord had called me to pastor, and he had been waiting for me to come to him. As the next couple weeks went by, I heard that scripture everywhere I went; so I located the scripture in the Bible. It was then that I knew for sure, God had spoken it to me.

Now, with the approval of my Bishop and a release in my spirit, my Bishop announced to the congregation that I was going out to pastor. Some of my spiritual brothers and sisters began to laugh at me and say things like— "She's done everything in the church but play an instrument and pastor; so I guess the instrument will be next", "God did not call her", "I wouldn't follow her to the bathroom". Others declared— "She's not married. God didn't call her." However, I obeyed the voice of the Lord and went to Raleigh, North Carolina and started door-to-door witnessing and let people know that I was starting a church; the doors began to open.

I was able to find a place called Fruit of Labor Culture Club where I would hold my Bible Study. One of my first members was an older white lady who was so sweet; she lived across the street from where I was holding Bible Study. Little did I know God was setting me up. This lady had a son who lived in Cincinnati, Ohio who had been diagnosed with a brain tumor. She was moving to live with him because she wanted to be there to take care of him.

She asked if I wanted to take over her place; it was a small strip of apartments and within that strip there were four families. As a result of this sweet lady living there, the four families became members of my church. My ministry began to grow and things were looking up.

One day a pastor came knocking at my door and asked for a minute of my time. He said he heard I was pastoring and felt that I shouldn't be because I was not married. My question to him was "what if I was married but my husband was not called into ministry to preach; did that mean I couldn't preach? I said, "This is crazy." He believed that I should bring my members and let them come to join his church.

This made me so upset I called my Bishop crying, and told him what happened. My Bishop said to me "Baby girl, you can always come back home". He knew this would put fire under me; he asked what I was going to do. I let him know I was going to pastor my church!

When people continued to say – "You can't pastor because you don't have a husband", I began to ask the Lord to give me an answer. God gave me an answer. So, I began to respond with these words– "If 5000 souls got saved by the mouth of a woman, do you think God would not accept them because they received Jesus Christ as their Lord and Savior through the mouth of a woman?"

With this people began to leave me alone; but I soon realized that people treat you differently as a single pastor. Sometimes, I would have to tell myself they don't accept you, but God accepts you. However, I felt like Rudolph the red-nosed reindeer: I was different.

I think about the biblical character, Hannah and how she endured humiliation and shame because she was barren. Hannah was ridiculed and tortured by Peninnah who had children, and was the other wife of Elkanah. Like Hannah, I was also treated badly in some circles. I was shamed because I didn't have a husband. This came from Christians: those who said they loved the Lord, but could not treat me as one of His children that he chose to use as a single pastor.

Hannah wanted a son and God wanted a prophet, the pain of not having a son drove her closer to God. Her perseverance in praying, made her a prayer warrior who became an overcomer; because the effectual fervent prayer of a righteous man (or woman) availeth much– James 5:6, KJV. Hannah remained barren until she poured her heart out to God in prayer and made a vow that she would allow her son to grow up in the temple. Hannah wanted a son and God had a plan for the life of that child. God needed the prophet: Samuel, the child to be. It had to happen! God blessed Hannah. She became the mother of three sons and two daughters.

It Had To Happen

After being divorced for almost thirteen years I met someone who I believed would love me for the rest of my life; he was also in the ministry and he swept me off my feet. I was in love and I finally felt like I was going to fit in with the married preachers. We went through premarital counseling, but something felt uneasy because I kept saying he has too many female friends.

My Bishop had gone on to be with the Lord, but his wife who loved me very much and was happy for what God was doing in my life, ministered to and counseled both of us.
When I expressed the uneasiness in my spirit, she said –"You don't have to go through with it; you can call the wedding off". However, because of the big announcement and all the money that had been spent, I married him.

I said I could handle anything but infidelity. Well, about six months into the marriage, my husband committed adultery. I was so hurt; but I tried everything I could to save my marriage. As the marriage was falling apart, we tried attending counseling, but it didn't work. The marriage was over.

This is not to bash my ex-husband or the woman involved in the infidelity. Rather, I share my story to help those of you that are reading this to understand that God is a healer. What you think you can't handle, God has already graced you to handle! I also want you to see that some of the things that happened in your life, God uses them to catapult you into your destiny. I am destined to win, I just had to push past the hurts and challenges.

As you can see my greatest fear became my reality, I kept telling people my husband was cheating on me, but his friends didn't believe me. Some of them cursed me out, called me crazy and told me that I should be ashamed of myself for lying on him. But when our divorce was final in March and he married the woman in April, just one month later, the truth was revealed, but the pain was greater.

Lord knows my three children had seen me go through a lot in earlier years! Of course they have always seen God pull me through. However, this pain was so public. It troubled me that my children were witnessing me experiencing such hurt. I knew that my pain was also causing my children to experience pain. My children had always seen me supporting others; I was always there for those in need. I know my children were thinking– why would God let this happen to our mom. See, your children know the real you and my children knew I had sold out for Christ. But it had to happen.

Some of my darkest days I spent watching the television show, Snapped; but I had to snap out of my darkness because I didn't want to see others miss what God had for them. I had to deal with my issues of abandonment, rejection, brokenness, and the ultimate question of– "what's wrong with me?" The pain was so great; I didn't think I would recover. But God!

Later, I realized it had to happen because there were other women who I knew who experienced unbelief at how things happened in their marriage or heartbreak over the death of loved ones. Now, they had seen me suffer through a failed marriage and not die in it. To the contrary, I came out a better and stronger woman of God. Gaining hope, they too came through as amazing, stronger women of God, and God did bless them!

There were days when all I could do was preach and then go home; my heart was broken and I felt like no one cared. Then one day I woke up and said, "The rest of the world is going on and my life is passing me by." I knew I had bounce- back ability as I had bounced back before, but the pain was so real. Pain forces you to get in the word of God; pain forces you to stop and look at how you got to that low valley place in your life.

The Healing Process

I pray this chapter revealed how I overcame rejection, humiliation and betrayal not only in Ministry but also in my divorce.

But instead of letting those experiences Stop me I use them to help other women who were facing similar struggles. Through my coaching program the winning approach I empowered women to break free from feeling stuck and start pursuing their dreams and goals again.

With my guidance, these women found the courage to go after what they wanted, come up with a solid plan and push through any obstacle that comes their way.

How did I get to this point? All because of my own experiences which gave me the resilience and determination to help others. let me tell you, there's no greater satisfaction than seeing someone rise from the sidelines and get back in the game of life

We must think forward in order to move forward: to deal with all the hurt and the shame. I realized I had survived the storm in my life, and I learned how to handle my emotions. There was purpose behind my pain. God had anointed me to handle all I had gone through and I could see that God really loved me. My life had purpose.

Having the right people in your life while you go through a storm is so important. When things happen, you need someone to help you get through them. You need people that will speak life when you can't pray and when you can't even cry. I really had a good support team, made up of people who really cared about me. It had to happen.

And then God began to really use me. I had forgiven my ex-husband and his new wife. I was now being used by God to tell my story of hurt, pain and now forgiveness. I was telling how I was healed because of the power and love of God. God was now getting the Glory out of my life. I preached love and not hate, and I began to receive countless testimonies from people expressing how my preaching of love and forgiveness had saved their lives. People were admitting to thoughts of wanting to kill others because of the pain they had experienced. Now, they rejoiced because they could let it go. Lives were saved, and people stayed out of jail. To God to be the Glory!

When we are hurt we put up walls, we draw back from others not knowing that is what the enemy wants us to do. But when the walls come down you realize you have to let go of people, past and present who have hurt you: not for them, but for you. Releasing them is setting you free.

Sometimes life changing experiences are really a setup:

Romans 8:28, "And we know that all things work together for good to them that love God, to them who are the called according to His purpose."

Ecclesiastes 3:1, "To everything there is a season, and a time to every purpose under the Heaven."

I was pushed into position, the pain changed the trajectory of my life, I was better not bitter. People would often say– "you are so strong", but there were days I did not want to be strong. People ask "are you okay?" Now, I can say– "I am better than okay, I have my life back and it is better than before. I am in a good place, I am healed and ready to love again; at one point I didn' t think I could ever love again."

The word says "blessed is she that believed for there shall be a performance of those things which were told her from the Lord!"

Blessed and highly favored that is me, for with God nothing shall be impossible! I went from tragedy to triumph, I survived it. To God be the Glory!

IT HAD TO HAPPEN!

Made in the USA
Columbia, SC
14 August 2023

21438423R10057